SOCIOLOGY
REINTERPRETED

Peter Berger is Professor of Sociology at Boston College. He is the author of *A Rumor of Angels, The Sacred Canopy, Invitation to Sociology, Pyramids of Sacrifice,* and *The Heretical Imperative,* among other books.

Hansfried Kellner is Professor of Sociology at the University of Darmstadt in West Germany.

SOCIOLOGY REINTERPRETED

An Essay on Method and Vocation

PETER L. BERGER

AND

HANSFRIED KELLNER

ANCHOR BOOKS
ANCHOR PRESS/DOUBLEDAY
Garden City, New York
1981

Sociology Reinterpreted: An Essay on Method and Vocation has been published simultaneously in hardcover and paperback editions.

Library of Congress Cataloging in Publication Data

Berger, Peter L.
  Sociology reinterpreted.

  Bibliography.
  Includes index.
  1. Sociology.   I. Kellner, Hansfried, joint author.
II. Title.
HM24.B393   301
ISBN: 0-385-17419-5
ISBN: 0-385-17420-9 (pbk.)
Library of Congress Catalog Card Number 80–2845

CONTENTS

CONTENTS

PREFACE

The intention of this book is simple: to restate, concisely and clearly, what the sociological approach to human reality essentially consists of. The term "method" refers not to the techniques of research employed by sociologists, but to the logic of their scientific investigations. The term "vocation," in line with a long usage, refers to an ethically self-conscious reflection about one's work. In other words, this book deals with what sociologists do and with what they are —and, since there are frankly hortatory aspects to the book, with what they *should* do and be. Thus we have not written an introduction to sociology here, nor a methodological treatise in the strict (philosophical) sense of the word, nor a survey of the "state of the art" (to use that phrase, which, for some curious reason, seems to have become fashionable of late). We have called our book "an essay" to describe its light, perhaps even easygoing character. It is a book intended to be read rather than pored over, and as we have had fun writing it, we have no objection if here and there the reader may be entertained as well as instructed.

We do not claim originality for the substance of our argument. It is a restatement of a central tradition in sociology, most directly identified with Max Weber, in our case strongly influenced by Alfred Schutz and other phenomenological writers. However, we have no wish to present here a sectarian manifesto, be it "Weberian" or "Schutzian." It is clear that not everyone will agree with us, but we have tried to steer away from intramural polemics as much as possible and to present a vision of sociology with which individuals from a number of different schools might agree.

Our motive for writing this book has come from our perception of the inordinate amount of confusion now reigning in the field as to some of its basic presuppositions and procedures. Perhaps one may also say that we have had a therapeutic, even pastoral motive in attempting to assuage some of the malaise that prevails among many colleagues. Our intended audience is broad, though we have mostly had younger colleagues in mind—younger faculty members, graduate students, the more thoughtful among undergraduate majors—those, in other words, in whom the future of sociology, if there is to be one, will be vested. The book may also be of interest to outsiders, especially in the other social sciences, who have quite similar problems. In any case, in writing the book we have not assumed that the reader will be deeply versed in the literature of sociology, though undoubtedly the reader with some familiarity with this literature will see aspects of our argument that others may miss. Those new to sociology may find some of the suggested readings in the appendix useful.

Brigitte Berger persuaded us that a book of this sort should be written. Otherwise preoccupied, she had to limit her participation in the writing of it to critical interest and moral encouragement, but both of these contributions have been invaluable throughout.

1

SOCIOLOGY AS A WAY
OF SEEING

It has often been observed that processes of change are greatly accelerated in the modern world. Quite often this seems to mean that institutions, groups and even individuals move rapidly from infantilism to senility with only the briefest intermediary period. Something like this appears to have happened to the discipline of sociology. Not so long ago—say, in the 1950s and even the early 1960s—the self-consciousness of sociologists was that of being members of a new and coming profession, while critics from the outside as well as from within berated sociology with this or that infantile disorder, be it in theory or methods or in the understanding of the discipline in the realm of the sciences. Today, by contrast, sociologists seem to spend an inordinate amount of time reassuring each other about the state of the profession, like inmates of a nursing home to whom it is a matter of mutual congratulation that they are still around at all.

Some of this demoralization, no doubt, has purely economic causes. Most sociologists are academically employed, and the severe economic troubles of academia inevitably affect the morale and self-consciousness of its denizens. There are also political troubles, stemming from the role played by sociologists in the *gauchisme* that has developed on the intellectual scene of Western Europe and North America since the late 1960s—a role that has been noted with less than enthusiastic admiration by other groups in those societies. But it is too easy to blame all the malaise in the field to the insolvency of the universities and the "reactionary" tendencies in the political system. At least some of this malaise is due to wide and deepening confusions within the field as to the proper understanding of what it means to do sociology. And this is a problem, largely self-inflicted, that can only be solved by a *prise de conscience* by sociologists as to their own vocation among the sciences and in the larger society.

The fact that sociology is not taken seriously by many outside it (including others within academia) would be easier to deal with if the same doubts had not infiltrated the ranks of sociologists themselves. Yet anyone hanging around the various gatherings of the discipline cannot fail to detect the self-doubts and the not always covert dissatisfaction with the fate of being a sociologist in this time. As always, self-doubt is more crippling than the doubts of outsiders.

This is not the place to deal with the economic and political context of contemporary sociology, or even with the place of the discipline in the precious pecking order of the academic ghetto. The topic of the present considerations is rather the proper self-understanding of the discipline itself. It may well be that the earlier self-confidence and the great expectations of sociologists were misguided. But so is the current demoralization. There is good reason for believing that sociology is and will continue to be a valid, even important, approach to the reality of human collective life. There is a need for clarity as to what sociology can and what it cannot do. One of the inherent qualities of sociology has been the sober acknowledgment of reality, the cutting through of illusions, including its own. This quality can be called upon today, and in this there is already hope for the future.

Sociology, from its beginnings, has been a very peculiar discipline, in that it discovered its object along with the methods of studying it: sociology was originally not just a new approach to the study of society, but it was part and parcel of the discovery of the phenomenon "society" as such. If one dates the beginnings of sociology from Auguste Comte, who invented the name of the discipline (perhaps appropriately mixing Latin and Greek in an inelegant neologism sure to offend every humanistic sensibility), this statement cannot be made without qualification: the phenomenon "society" was perceived and analyzed before Comte. But, as Albert Salomon has shown, it is arbitrary to date sociology in this way. It makes much more sense to understand the discipline so named in the early nineteenth century as one particular step in the development of a perspective that, at least as far back as the seventeenth century, can quite properly be called sociological. Sociology, then, differs in a very interesting way from other sciences. Obviously it differs from the physical sciences: the physical universe was perceived before modern physics, life was known before modern biology and so on. But sociology differs in this respect even from other human sciences: thus the economy was known as a phenomenon before modern economics, the political order before modern political science, and so on. What is more, insofar as the modern approaches to these phenomena differ from earlier ones, they do so precisely to the degree that they came to share in the sociological perspective in the broad sense.

At the heart of the modern sociological perspective is the perception of the autonomous and frequently covert dynamics of human collective entities. "Society" is nothing but a name for whatever "works away," by rules that were yet to be discovered, "underneath" the collective structures as they were "officially" defined by such normative disciplines as theology, philosophy and law. It follows that to be able to perceive "society" at all there must be a certain debunking angle of vision. It follows further that sociology was a way of seeing the world as soon as it found its object of inquiry, and all later elaborations of this peculiar vision are a sort of unpacking of what was already implied in that first act of perception. Thus, in twentieth-century American sociology, Robert Merton coined the terms "manifest" and "latent functions" to designate, respectively, the "officially defined" purposes of a particular institution or social arrangement and the "underlying" (and *ipso facto* unperceived or unconscious) purposes that the sociologist is in a position to disclose. For example, the "manifest" function of education is to transmit knowledge, its "latent" function to erect and maintain class barriers; or, hospitals "manifestly" are organized to treat illness, "latently" to preserve and enforce the status prerogatives of physicians; and so on. But to be able to say any of these things presupposes a very peculiar angle of vision to begin with, which is of the essence of sociology: underneath the visible edifices of the human world there is a hidden, invisible structure of interests and forces waiting to be uncovered by the sociologist. The "manifest" is not the whole story; "latency" is there to be studied. Or, in the simplest terms, *the world is not what it appears to be.*

In this debunking quality of sociology lies its intrinsically subversive character. Any collective order is always legitimated by official definitions, and the demonstration that the latter tell only a part of the story or, worse, serve to obfuscate what really goes on, is intrinsically subversive of "good order." In other words, sociology begins to "subvert" from the first moment that it applies to social reality its peculiar way of seeing. It is very important to emphasize that this is so *regardless* of whether a particular sociologist *intends* to subvert. Indeed, the great figures of the classical period of sociology—Emile Durkheim, Max Weber, Vilfredo Pareto—can all be described as conservative in one way or another, and except for the Marxists most sociologists have been, at the most, mild reformists rather than revolutionaries. Nevertheless, however "conservative" their intentions, the thought of these sociologists has had a deeply unsettling quality that disturbed and angered those with a stake in having things appear as "officially defined." The relation of sociology to political action is a topic to be covered later, but one point can already be made here: *Sociologists are always at odds with their own discipline if they want to play the role of advocates*—or, more precisely, if they want to do so *qua* sociologists. This is true regardless of whether they advocate "conservative" or "revolutionary" causes. The genius of sociology is negative; and, paradoxically, it is as negation that sociology can make its best contribution to any positive cause. The "subversive" quality of sociology has always been sensed, almost instinctively, by dictatorial regimes of every ideological coloration, which is why sociology is either repressed or becomes a caricature of itself in countries governed by such regimes.

There is, of course, the fascinating historical question of why this perspective developed in Europe at a particular time—a question that cannot be pursued here in detail. One reason frequently given is the rapidity of social change brought on by capitalism and by the industrial revolution in modern Europe. But there have been periods of rapid social change in other places, in earlier times, without this particular consequence. One may follow Max Weber here, in hypothetizing that an important factor was the peculiar Western rationality, rooted all the way back in biblical religion, Hellenic reason and Roman law—the same Western rationality, indeed, that made possible the cataclysmic transformations of modern capitalism and modern technology. There can be no doubt that the sociological perspective is founded on this rationality, which is why the discipline from its inception understood itself as *a science* (though, of course, there were different interpretations of just what that meant—as between, for example, the French and German classics in the field). This self-understanding, however, has always stood in a certain tension with the "debunking" or negative thrust of the sociological perspective, for it implied the *makability* of the world: *Not only is the world not what it appears to be, but it could be different from what it is*. In other words, most sociologists (even those as pessimistic as Weber) were always tempted to apply their insights to the rational "betterment" of society—an application that led them to the aforementioned ambiguity, of being debunkers in the role of advocates. This "tinkering" motive in sociology is, of course, its linkage to the ideals of the Enlightenment, to the aspiration of establishing a more rational and supposedly more humane social order. This motive became all the more urgent in the context of secularization. As the religious norms for a "right order" paled in plausibility, it became all the more important to reorder human affairs in a rational manner. In this, needless to say, sociology has been part of a much broader movement of the Western mind, as have all the other social sciences and generally social thought since the seventeenth century.

The twentieth century has inflicted some severe shocks to Enlightenment optimism and to the very notion of the rational "makability" of the world. Indeed, it could be argued that both modernity and modern secular rationality are today in a state of crisis. This too is very likely related to the malaise within sociology. Some may wish to reaffirm the optimistic faith of the Enlightenment, be it by way of Marxist "progressivism" or through more centrist-liberal versions of the idea of progress (as, for instance, Robert Nisbet has recently done, in the best Durkheimian tradition). Such reaffirmation is not the position taken here. Those who feel unable to return to an Enlightenment faith and to the concomitant hopes for the fruits of "applied" sociology find themselves precisely in Max Weber's predicament: this is the predicament of one who tries to see the world as lucidly as possible, who suffers from the radical "disenchantment" such lucidity almost invariably brings about—and who *nevertheless* is committed to humanizing interventions, political or otherwise, in the course of collective events. In this is to be found the first reason for Weber's continuing relevance for the called-for *prise de conscience* of sociology.

There is another reason why Weber is a logical focus for contemporary sociologists as they seek to rediscover the inner genius of their discipline—to wit, his obsession with the question of the nature of modernity. In this too Weber is representative of the sociological enterprise as a whole. For sociology is not only a peculiarly modern discipline in its approach and methods; it has also been transfixed from the beginning by modernity as a topic of inquiry. These have been core questions for all the great sociologists, before, during and since the classical period of the discipline: How is the modern world different? How did it get that way? What are its essential structures? Where is it going? These questions, of course, were focal for Weber in his entire opus—but they were equally focal for Durkheim, Pareto, Georg Simmel, Thorstein Veblen and Talcott Parsons, and indeed for Karl Marx. Sociology cannot forget these questions without losing a core element of its intellectual substance.

The focus on modernity implies an effort to see contemporary society as a whole, in itself and in relation to other societies. That is, it implies that the sociological perspective is comprehensive and comparative. Put negatively, all parochial approaches in sociology entail a loss of intellectual substance. This is certainly not to say that there is no validity in sociological investigations that deal with the minutiae of human behavior in some particular corner of one's own society, without immediate reference to any attempt to understand that society as a whole or in comparison with other societies. Good sociologists have always had an insatiable curiosity about even the trivialities of human behavior, and if this curiosity leads a sociologist to devote many years to the painstaking exploration of some small corner of the social world that may appear quite trivial to others, so be it: Why do more teenagers pick their noses in rural Minnesota than in rural Iowa? What are the patterns of church socials over a twenty-year period in small-town Saskatchewan? What is the correlation between religious affiliation and accident-proneness among elderly Hungarians? Far be it from us to denigrate such research interests! Indeed, we find it reassuring, even inspiring, that there are sociological colleagues who not only dedicate themselves to such projects but are able to generate considerable passion in doing so! One might even argue that there is a moral quality in the capacity of the sociologist to devote careful attention to the trivia of human life; this is a sort of sociological footnote to the old adage that "nothing human is alien to me"—and that, consequently, nothing human is too humble for my respectful attention! All the same, there would be something seriously wrong if the *entire* discipline lost itself in pursuits of such provincial scope.

Put differently, *sociology must return to the "big questions."* Paramount among these questions, today as during the classical period, are the aforementioned ones about the constitution of the modern world. For better or for worse, they have not been answered once and for all. What is more, everyday brings new evidence and new material for the enterprise of answering them. Sociology as a discipline, then, cannot but try to regain ever again a vision of the whole of contemporary society—more or less what Marcel Mauss once called *le fait social total.* And this means that sociologists must retain some ability for cross-cultural, global comparisons, in historical depth as well as in contemporary terms. Put simply, the calling of sociologist is by its very nature a cosmopolitan one. Conversely, the provincialism of much sociological training (let the inability of most American sociologists today to operate in any language other than English be merely mentioned here) is something badly in need of revision.

To sum up some of the foregoing: A revitalization of sociology will mean above all a revitalization of a certain perspective, of a way of seeing the world. In this, it is the contention here, Max Weber's work continues to be of strategic importance. But let it be quickly added that what is being proposed here is by no means a "return to Weber" in the sense of setting up a dogmatic authority (we are quite content to leave such scholastic exercises to those Marxists who thrive on them). Sociology is a science, not a set of doctrines, and its own sources must never be immune to its debunking propensity. Nor is it a question of "returning to Weber" in a spirit of reactionary nostalgia. Rather, it is a matter of returning to the intellectual sources nourishing this particular discipline. It is clear that the present situation, both socially and intellectually, is very different from Weber's, so that no simple "return" is possible even if one should desire such a thing.

Still, why Weber? As has already been shown, there are several answers to this, but the most important answer is probably this: Because Weber, more than any other figure in the history of the discipline, had a passionate and enduring dedication to the task of clarifying just what the sociological way of seeing is. It is this, much more than any specifics of Weber's sociology, that present-day sociologists should "return" to—that is, not so much return to Weber as to the "spirit of Weberianism." While Weber was undoubtedly committed to the scientific rationality of the modern West, he had a very distinctive understanding of what this meant for the study of human affairs: human phenomena don't speak for themselves; they must be *interpreted*. Thus a clarification of the act of interpretation was at the center of Weber's methodology. This clarification, though, involved more than arid methodological considerations. It had a moral, even a humane dimension. There is a particular existential attitude in patiently, carefully being attentive to the meanings of other people's lives, to the "deciphering" of the inner meanings of social phenomena. Implied in this attitude is a respect for other people and their intentions, hopes and ways of life. Implied further is the determination to see the social world as it is, regardless of one's own wishes and fears—that is, to separate what *is* from what one believes *ought to be*. Thus Weber's approach has implications for the *vocation* of sociology as well as for its *method*. Despite the dry character of so much of Weber's methodological work, this explains the paradoxical fact that it has the capacity to inspire as well as to instruct.

In the just-mentioned qualities Weber differs significantly from other figures and streams in the development of sociology. Emile Durkheim, and with him the whole school of French sociology founded by him, evinces a very different spirit. It is a spirit much closer to that of the Enlightenment. Thus his method remains essentially positivistic, akin to the natural sciences. Although society is very clearly understood as a reality *sui generis,* the method of sociology is finally not determined by this quality of society but by an abstract concept of what science ought to be. Also in unbroken continuity with the Enlightenment, Durkheim did not undergo the disjunction between the "is" and the "ought" of social reality; throughout his work there is, if one may put it this way without seeming disrespectful, an easy nexus between the two. This same lack of clarity about the boundaries between scientific understanding and normative judgment has been transmitted from Durkheim to the various "functionalist" traditions in Anglo-American social science. Although there have been disclaimers of this implication by the leading figures in these traditions (such as Talcott Parsons and Robert Merton in this country), all too often there has been the notion that the demonstration that something is "functional" in a particular "social system" *ipso facto* bestows some sort of positive normative judgment. As to the Marxist tradition in sociology, here, though in a manner very different from Durkheim's, there is a similar erosion of the line between the "is" and the "ought" of society. In the case of Marxism, of course, the reason for this is *not* a positivistic ideal of science. Rather, it is because society is seen under the aspect of a philosophy of history, to the point where scientific understanding is deemed impossible (or rather, distortive) except as an integral part of this philosophical procedure. At the end of the procedure stands a utopian vision of the future, without which the entire procedure loses its plausibility.

All of these points will have to be discussed in much greater detail in later chapters. But already now it is possible to state very generally the understanding of sociological work, not so much in "Weber's" terms as in a "Weberian spirit." This understanding avoids *both* the positivistic *and* the utopian versions of the sociological enterprise. It is understood that no scientific method can deal with all of human reality in a comprehensive and ultimately unproblematic way. Rather, science always views its objects in a selective, partial and *ipso facto* problematic manner. This is even true of all perceptions of society as a whole; in Weberian terms, even *"le fait social total"* is itself a construct of the observing scientist (in fairness it ought to be stated that Marcel Mauss would probably not have approved of this Weberian qualification of his phrase). Most importantly, science can never provide moral guidelines for action. But the same understanding also precludes any form of utopianism, which sees the present as leading up to an inevitable and redemptive future. If science cannot provide a morality, even less can it provide a doctrine of salvation. This understanding of science, and of sociology as a science, finally clarifies the difference between intellectual analysis and existence, between reflection and sheer living. There are hard dividing lines between these domains of the human condition. One may deplore these, even consider them "alienating." But one cannot easily jump over them.

Positivism and utopianism, in various "denominational" forms, are today the two dominant camps in sociology. The mix is somewhat different in different countries (thus positivism is probably still the larger camp in North America, while utopianism is more powerful in Western Europe and in the Third World), and there are all sorts of quarrels between the "denominations." The position taken here, however, is that in the last analysis *both* positivism *and* utopianism represent aberrations of the sociological enterprise, and that a revitalization of the discipline will have to bring about a conscious, fully thought through repudiation of both. Once more, it is worth stressing that this involves vocation as well as method—that is, it involves not only an understanding of the cognitive structure of this particular discipline, but an understanding of what it means *to be a sociologist*. There is a vocation of thinking through and living through the tensions between "is" and "ought," between understanding and hope, between scientific analysis and action. Both positivism and utopianism offer shortcuts, easy ways out of the tensions, be it in the role of the "mere scientist" who denies the normative dilemmas or in the role of the prophet who supposedly has the final resolutions of these dilemmas up his sleeve. Both of these shortcuts, it is not too difficult to see, provide psychological relief, and this fact probably accounts to a large degree for their enduring attractiveness.

It is also quite possible that this same vacillation between positivism and utopianism is a factor in the widespread public reluctance to take sociology seriously. The public is disillusioned with "mere scientists," whose recommendations are "merely technical," and *ipso facto* avoid the moral agonies of so many social problems. But the public may also have learned to be suspicious of sociologists wearing the mantle of prophecy (the same sociologists, of course, who always claim to be *more than* "mere technicians"): all too often the prophecies have turned out to be false—or, worse, have been revealed to be self-serving. A proper understanding of what sociology can and what it cannot do will lead to greater care in giving advice to the public and to various institutions. It will lead to a careful eschewing of dogmatism of any variety. Just possibly, such modesty will regain a measure of public respect, and at the same time diminish the uncertainty among sociologists themselves as to the validity of what they are doing.

The world today is very different from what it was in Weber's lifetime. The process of "rationalization," which Weber (correctly) perceived as the innermost force of modernity, is still developing vigorously, and indeed has now become a truly global phenomenon. But (as Weber foresaw but did not live to see) there are now powerful countermovements. Put differently, in many parts of the world, and definitely in Western Europe and North America, one can observe today a dialectic between modernization and countermodernization. Put in Weberian terms, there continues to be widespread "disenchantment," but there are also powerful movements of "re-enchantment"—religious, cultural and political. Also, the split between private life and the mega-institutions of the public realm has become much deeper, and so, concomitantly, has the sense of alienation among various groups of people.

Sociology, and all the social sciences, cannot avoid being caught up in these developments. Sociologists have been caught up on both sides of the modernization/countermodernization divide. The "mere scientists," needless to say, have always been modernizers at heart. Positivism, in the spirit of the Enlightenment, implies a modernizing attitude. It is all the more noteworthy, though, that it is precisely individuals with a positivistic understanding of sociology who are very vulnerable to conversions to this or that counter-modernizing faith: since their conception of science is no help at all in discriminating between different redemptive creeds, their critical faculties often collapse suddenly and totally when their existential troubles reach a certain degree of intensity. Other sociologists have allied themselves from the beginning with various attempts to "re-enchant" the world, typically in terms of this or that "countercultural" movement. Their reputation as sociologists has then been invested totally in the fate of these movements. All these attempts involve prophecy, messianism, be it in terms of private or political programs. And all these attempts vastly overburden sociology; that is, they imply an understanding of what sociology is capable of doing that greatly exceeds its real capacities, and thus inevitably leads to frustration and disappointment. As the crisis of the social order has become deeper and, in places, more cataclysmic, these failures of sociology have inevitably led to disillusion both within the discipline and in the broader public. It follows that a *reprise de conscience* of sociology will, perhaps more than anything else, involve a *recognition of limits*.

To repeat: What is at issue here is not, cannot be, a simple reiteration of some lost wisdom from the classical age of sociology. Thus it cannot be a matter of becoming some sort of orthodox Weberian. Consequently, in the following chapters other, non-Weberian sources are constantly used to delineate the proper character of the sociological enterprise. Let some of them be merely mentioned here: phenomenological analysis, especially as developed by Alfred Schutz; the sociology of knowledge; the American tradition deriving from George Herbert Mead, leading to a much greater awareness than Weber had of the interface of social-psychological and institutional analysis; and generally an interest in microsociological patterns, which are important even if one is ultimately interested in the "big questions." Perhaps enough has been said, though, to obviate the suspicion that what is being proposed here is some sort of sociological neo-orthodoxy.

But back to the beginning of this chapter: Sociology, whatever else it may be, is a very peculiar way of seeing the human world. A necessary focus of the present considerations, then, must be the careful clarification of just what this way of seeing is. The next step, then, must be such a clarification of the act of sociological interpretation, that act which Weber called *Verstehen*, and with which the whole sociological enterprise must stand or fall.

2

THE ACT
OF INTERPRETATION

All human beings have meaning and seek to live in a meaningful world. In principle, every human meaning is accessible to others. Indeed, this mutual accessibility is a decisive premise for the belief that there is something like a shared humanity. But, of course, some meanings are more accessible than others. Following the distinctions made by Alfred Schutz, two broad kinds of meanings may be distinguished: There are the meanings within the individual's own life-world, those that are actually or potentially "within reach" or "at hand," and that are usually self-understood in the natural attitude of everyday living. And then there are the meanings *outside* the individual's own life-world, meanings of other societies or less familiar sectors of one's own society, also meanings from the past; these are all meanings that are not immediately available in the natural attitude, are not "within reach" or "at hand," but rather must be appropriated through specific processes of initiation, be it through immersing oneself in a different social context or (especially in the case of meanings from the past) through specific intellectual disciplines. Further distinctions must be made: in all the aforementioned cases, there is a difference between the ordinary interpretation of meanings in everyday life and interpretations in terms of the social sciences. Further: one must distinguish between interpreting the meanings of individuals with whom one is in actual or potential face-to-face interaction (those whom Schutz called "consociates"), the meanings of individuals with whom such interaction is *not* taking place (called "contemporaries"—or, in the case of the past, "predecessors"), and finally meanings that are embodied in anonymous structures (such as the meaning of an institution with whose concrete human representatives no interaction may ever take place).

Even the reader not familiar with the more arcane zones of the Schutzian corpus will readily see that all of this can quickly get to be very complicated. Rather than spin out the complexities, let us immediately apply them to a concrete example. In other words, let us see how interpretation actually occurs in concrete social situations. As phenomenologists like to say, let us construct a world—or, in this instance, at least a miniworld:

I am a young woman, a graduate student of sociology in a less than elite state university in the Middle West. I am attending a sociology convention in a big hotel on the West Coast. Right now, in between sessions, I am engaged in conversation with another young woman, a graduate student at an elite university in California. We have been talking about (what else?) the job market and she has been giving me some interesting and potentially useful information about job openings in her part of the country. The conversation has been friendly, animated, and both in form and content very familiar to me—that is, although I have just met this particular individual, I have had such conversations before on quite a few occasions, and although some of the information conveyed by her is new and interesting to me, none of it is surprising. Then, suddenly and without warning, an element of stark, indeed alarming unfamiliarity is injected into the conversation, a big surprise that abruptly changes the placid quality of the interchange. My conversation partner looks at her watch, apologizes, and says that she must really go now. I mumble something by way of regretful assent. She has already started to move away, turns back, gives me a searching look, and says: "I don't really know you at all. Perhaps I shouldn't say this. But some friends of mine from L.A. are having an orgy, up on the fourteenth floor. I'm sure they would be happy if you came along. I think we could use an additional woman. Why don't you come with me? Some of the men are really very nice."

Now, let us freeze this tableau for a moment. Just what is happening now? Never mind for now whether I'm shocked or titillated, tempted to accept the invitation or to quickly retreat from the encounter. This has never happened to me before and, quite apart from my feelings and from what I might eventually do about the situation, what is happening right now is clear and simple: *I have been presented with a communication that calls out for interpretation.* Indeed, as soon as I have recovered from the steep upsurge in my adrenalin level, a number of different possible interpretations are crowding into my mind: "This is a joke." Or: "This is not really an invitation to an orgy, but an attempt at lesbian seduction." Or even: "Maybe I didn't hear right?" Each one of these possible interpretations would, if given credence, pull the situation back from outrageous unfamiliarity into the safety of the familiar —some people have a somewhat strange sense of humor; I have been approached by lesbians before;

some of these Californians do talk a little funny. Let us further assume, though, that I dismiss the afore-mentioned interpretations——there is nothing to indicate that she is joking; lesbians bent on seduction do not mention nice men; Californian or not, she was speaking standard American English, and there is nothing wrong with my hearing. I conclude, therefore, that the com-munication says what it seems to say: I am indeed being invited to an orgy. This conclusion presents me, in a very concrete way, with a social world that is new to me. However I will eventually respond to this world, on the level of further actions, I'm also being presented with an intellectual challenge. I must, as it were, ex-pand my cognitive map to incorporate this new item of social reality.

To say that I must expand my cognitive map is an-other way of saying that I must find a way of interpret-ing the new territory that I have just discovered. In other words, interpretation is also a kind of incorpo-ration: I move to understand the new by relating it to the old in my own experience. Now, it so happens in this case, I don't have to start from scratch. Although such a communication has never been made to me be-fore, it does fit into things I know or believe to know—about Californian life-styles, for one (I have read Cyra McFadden's *Serial;* I've even seen the movie). If I can do this credibly, what I'm doing is to subsume the new information under a cognitive rubric that is already "at hand": "So Californians *really* behave this way!" In that case, while the concrete situation is indeed new to me, my cognitive apparatus already contains the cate-gories by which the situation can be incorporated into my view of the social world. One could also say, then, that the situation is new, but not *all that* new. (To bring this point home, imagine a different invitation: "Some friends of mine from L.A. are having a blood sacrifice, up on the fourteenth floor. We don't have the victim yet. Would you like to be it? . . .") But even though I can now subsume the new information under categories already available to me, minimally I must reconstruct these categories to accommodate what has just occurred: the phrase "They *really* behave this way!" already constitutes such a reconstruction. As I continue to talk with my conversation partner, the reconstruction is likely to become firmer and more elaborate.

Now, it is important to stress that, in this example, I have not entered this conversation in the course of a sociological research project; indeed, up to now my reactions have been altogether similar to those of an ordinary person not blessed with any training in sociology. The intellectual effort at understanding what is being said to me then does not proceed systematically, step by step. Rather, it seems to happen spontaneously, with whole chunks of information being rapidly absorbed and "worked into" my cognitive system. This ongoing activity of interpretation is taking place within my own mind while the external conversation is going on; that is, my interpretation takes place in an inner conversation, which is a crucial *sotto voce* accompaniment to the verbal exchanges. But it is time to push our little story one step ahead. After the invitation has been issued to me, and after I have concluded that it is indeed what it purports to be (a conclusion that I will have reached in a fraction of the time needed here to put its logic on paper), I don't respond to it right away, either positively or negatively. *My interest has been aroused.* And (even if this may be in part to gain a little time) I begin to ask questions: Who are these friends from L.A.? Do they often do this? Does my conversation partner participate often? Just what goes on at these events? And so on.

At this point, of course, I am doing much more than interpreting the meaning of a single communication by another person. I have begun an investigation that will allow me to interpret a larger, perhaps much larger, segment of the social world. This, still, need not be a properly sociological investigation; the questions I ask now are those that any ordinary individual whose interest is aroused would ask. These questions, then, need not issue from some logic of systematic inquiry, and they follow each other without much forethought and in no planned sequence. But, if my partner is ready to answer them, they will naturally enable me to embark on a much more comprehensive interpretation of the phenomenon. If this is to be the result, though, there is a simple but exceedingly important presupposition: *I must listen.*

Again in very ordinary terms, it is not hard to spell out what is involved in this: I must keep attentive to what this person is saying. I must not let my mind wander, and I must try to keep attuned to her communications. I must not interrupt. And I must especially not interrupt with judgments or opinions of my own, not only because this might make her angry or defensive, but because it will deflect my attention from what she is communicating to me. That is, I must try to control my impulses of distraction or emotional affect (positive *or* negative). All of this adds up to a willingness to be open-minded at least for the moment: in order to grasp her view of the world, I must bracket my own for at least as long as this exploratory conversation is going on.

Let us suppose that this effort at a more ample understanding has been successful. My conversation partner has delayed her departure for the delights of the fourteenth floor long enough to answer my questions. What has happened now is that, minimally, I have acquired firsthand knowledge about people who conduct orgies at scholarly conventions. However modestly, this has modified my cognitive map in terms of this particular feature—if you will, my cognitive map of the sexual mores of American society. The very fact that my interest has been aroused (a possibility, let it be noted, even if unaccompanied by any arousal of the libido whatever) implies that this new knowledge is relevant to me. Putting this in more precise Schutzian terms, what I have done in this act of interpretation is to accommodate my own *relevance structure* to that of this other person and of the group with which she is affiliated.

The longer this conversation goes on, the more elaborate will be this accommodation of relevance structures. I will get to know more about her and her friends' general view of the world—which will in all likelihood include matters not directly related to sexuality. Indeed, I will begin to obtain an understanding of a general view of the world *within which* these sexual practices make sense to these people. This general view is likely to include some sort of a theory of interpersonal relations, of intimacy, perhaps of politics, or of religion. As I continue to question, my questions will be the result of an ongoing correlation between what I already know, what I am finding out now and what I would like to find out. Very likely, this gathering stock of knowledge will allow me to "locate" this particular woman more exactly within some set of social categories—that is, I will *typify* her. Thus, for example, I will be able to go beyond classifying her as "a Californian" (an obviously imprecise typification when it comes to people who participate in orgies—think of all those Reagan voters!), but instead will be in the process of constructing a much more detailed type of person who engages in such activities.

Remember this, though: my own construction of this type is dependent on what she has been telling me. Put differently: it is *she* who is giving me a portrait of this sexual subculture—we haven't gone to the fourteenth floor, not yet anyway—we're still down here in the coffee shop! Thus there are two hypotheses emerging from the conversation. One: the type of person represented by this individual perceives this subculture in this particular way. Or two: her perception of the subculture is a valid one. If I am to choose between the two hypotheses, I must obviously, by whatever means, come to some sort of conclusion as to my informant's *reliability*. Depending on which choice I make, I will say one of two things (say to myself, that is): "I now understand how, perhaps why, this person perceives the world in this way"; or, "This is a perception I ought to take seriously" (not necessarily seriously in the sense of wanting to join her subculture, but of acknowledging that her account of it is valid). One can use two terms of Jean Piaget's here: in the first instance, I have *assimilated* her point of view—that is, I have absorbed it into my own viewpoint, which has not changed very much in consequence; in the second instance, I have *accommodated* my point of view to hers, thus changing the former substantially. In either case, though, I see the world differently now. Put simply: *I cannot interpret another's meaning without changing, albeit minimally, my own meaning system.*

To repeat: thus far, in this example, I have been in this situation as an individual with an interest in understanding an unaccustomed slice of social reality just presented to me, but not *qua* sociologist; everything said so far about my efforts at interpretation could also have been said if I were, say, a buyer for a Midwestern department store, or a housewife, or (these days at least) a nun. But let us now vary the example slightly: I am now in this same conversation *qua* sociologist— that is, my efforts are now directed toward a specifically sociological interpretation. To say that I'm in the conversation *qua* sociologist may mean one of two things: either, let us imagine, that I have been hanging around the coffee shop with precisely this research interest in mind—I'm writing my doctoral dissertation about the sexual mores of sociologists— presumably, then, we will also have to imagine that the aforesaid invitation to an orgy was not an altogether fortuitous event but was sought out and perhaps provoked by me in the pursuit of my research. Or, alternatively, we can leave the situation as previously described but simply imagine that, in the course of the conversation, my interest *as a sociologist* is aroused— that is, inwardly if not verbally, I now define myself as a sociologist engaged in doing research on an unexpectedly interesting situation. What changes as a result of this switch from ordinary participant to sociological investigator?

As a sociologist I must certainly continue to listen and to interpret, but both the listening and the interpreting now take on a peculiar character. The similarities with ordinary listening and interpreting are great; essentially the same procedures as those just described will continue to take place. But the differences are important, and they can be spelled out. To begin with, I now establish a greater kind of *distance* from the situation within my own mind. Deliberately, I step outside the situation, take on the role of an outsider (even if the other partner in the situation is not aware of my detachment). By the same token, this distancing right away gives me a greater sense of control over what is taking place. It is still essential that I retain an open mind in listening, but this *ad hoc* (or *pro tem*) open-mindedness is more systematic and disciplined than that of the ordinary listener. And, of course, if I have done sociological research before, I have acquired habits of listening in this way that will be "at hand" for me as soon as I define this particular situation as a research occasion. I will also have developed a habit of disengaging my own existential concerns from the situation as far as I'm able—in the example, say, moral disapproval or breathless libidinal excitement or the quasi-religious expectation that I'm on the brink of a salvific insight or experience—and I will look upon the situation as one in which such disengagement is appropriate (as against, say, a conversation with my fiancé or my husband, when a comparable disengagement of existential concerns would not only be inappropriate but a betrayal of the personal relationship).

As I explore the situation sociologically, there is also the previously described interaction of my own relevance structure with that of my conversation partner and, hopefully, with the relevance structure of the sexual subculture that is coming into view as a result of her communications. But my own relevance structure now is not only more systematic and explicit; it is a relevance structure *of a different kind*. This is because it has not been shaped merely by my own previous experiences and interpretations, but by the body of sociological theory and knowledge, and this lore of the discipline is constantly present in my own process of interpretation. The typifications and hypotheses that I now undertake are also both more systematic and different in content. For instance, in typifying my conversation partner and her circle of friends I may pay special attention to their *class*, and in doing this I bring into my interpretation an entire body of stratification theory and data derived from the work of other sociologists. Thus I may hypothesize, on the basis of studies made by this or that other sociologist, that this sexual pattern is typical of upwardly mobile lower-middle-class Evangelical Protestants whose parents are divorced—or (what the hell) downwardly mobile upper-middle-class Jews who suffered from hay fever in their teens. Put differently: as I interpret the situation, *sotto voce* in my role as sociologist, the entire discipline (or, rather, that segment of it that is theoretically relevant to this research material) is invisibly present in my own mind—a silent partner in the situation, as it were.

As a trained sociologist, I can readily draw upon a large body of knowledge without doing this explicitly step by step. In other words, this whole body of knowledge is at hand for me. Almost automatically there flash before my mind different *possible* interpretations of this particular situation. The decision as to which of these I will actually apply will depend on its "fit" with the data in question. I do this spontaneously and implicitly. At the moment, however, that the data do *not* seem to "fit" into one of these available schemes of interpretation, I will now turn to an explicit and systematic comparison of possible interpretations. At this point, I am, as it were, "juggling" a number of possible interpretations. If none of them "fits" sufficiently, I will then be constrained to construct a *new,* or at least greatly modified, interpretation of my own. In doing this, I make a deliberate effort to sort out, or "falsify," what is already known as against the new knowledge I'm attempting to acquire. This is a deliberate undertaking of construction. This point will be returned to below in the discussion of conceptualization. Suffice it to point out now that this procedure is a safeguard against becoming dogmatic (in the sense of adhering to my previous point of view and forcing the data into it) and also against overlooking certain data that do not subsume themselves readily under previously available schemes of interpretation.

Also, as a sociologist I have a different way of dealing with the possible validity of what this individual has been saying. On the spot, having typified her, I can immediately hypothesize that others of her type are likely to hold these particular views. But if I want to decide whether to accommodate these views into my own sociological perception of American sexual mores, there is only one course of action for me to pursue: *I must go out and do further research into this putative subculture.* This need not necessarily mean that I follow my conversation partner to the fourteenth floor to see whether there really is an orgy and whether it is what she has claimed it to be; it means even less that, having gone to the fourteenth floor, I now participate in the sexual goings-on. I might indeed, in the interest of science, decide to be a so-called participant-observer; in that case it will be all the more important to maintain some inner detachment from the situation, difficult though this may be (it has been determined that orgasm and stratification theory do not mix easily). Or, if they let me, I might decide to remain an observer, engaged in what an earlier generation of Catholics was advised to do when inescapably trapped in non-Catholic religious observances—"inconspicuous non-participation" (this too may be difficult at an orgy). But, of course, there are other avenues open to me. I can interview other likely informants. I can seek contact with the subculture under other conditions that may be more favorable to research. If funded, I can hire other people to do the research for me. But, whatever avenue of research I finally choose to follow, it is clear that the validity or invalidity of this individual's report will have to be subjected to a process of (in principle rigorous) *empirical testing.* Conversely, I cannot draw any conclusions about the matter of validity simply on the basis of whether this individual seems credible to me—let alone on the basis of *a priori* theoretical convictions of mine. *All* my hypotheses—about downwardly mobile Protestants, hay-fever-afflicted Jewish teenagers, and so on—will be subject to this process of empirical testing. And, if my research is honest, I must remain open to the possibility that some of the hypotheses will not be supported by my findings.

What we have described so far is the interpretation (be it in ordinary life or *qua* sociologist) of meanings presented in face-to-face interaction. However, meanings are also presented by anonymous means, where concrete other persons are not empirically available. For example, I may be sitting at home, reading a newspaper story about new sexual mores in California. If I want to interpret this story, how is this act of interpretation different from the previously described face-to-face conversation? Again, there are many similarities, but the differences are important. In the newspaper a view of the world is being presented to me in a highly organized way, as against the much looser presentation in conversation. Most people, after all, do not speak in carefully ordered paragraphs. This also means that this particular item of alleged information is placed in a wider context—minimally, in the context of what the editors of this newspaper consider to be news —but possibly also in the context of the newspaper's wider presentation of social reality. Thus, for example, this may be a conservative newspaper, and this particular story is part of an ongoing depiction of the degeneracy of American society; or, on the contrary, this is a newspaper sympathetic to the cultural revolutions of the age, in which case the story may be part of a series of reports from the frontiers of liberation.

Also, in reading the newspaper, I can "listen" to its view of the world, in the sense of being attentive to it and trying to be open-minded. But I cannot ask questions. Therefore, the interlocking between my own body of knowledge and that presented to me is more difficult. I cannot so readily (using George Herbert Mead's phrase) "take the role of the other" in trying to penetrate into an unfamiliar cognitive map. Consequently, what the newspaper presents to me lacks the immediacy of what William James called the "accent of reality"; it is much easier to "put down" (in *both* senses of the phrase) the newspaper than a person sitting across the table. If I read the newspaper *qua* sociologist—newspaper stories then are part of my "data"—I have one slight advantage: I can more easily withdraw from the situation and confront the knowledge presented by the newspaper with my own body of knowledge. Put differently, the newspaper cannot as easily "suck me into" this new viewpoint as can an individual who is in face-to-face interaction with me. But if I now want to interpret the newspaper story as a sociologist, I must also be very much on my guard—precisely because of the highly organized form of the presentation. Unlike the face-to-face conversation, the newspaper presents its view to me in what could be called a *protoscientific* form—that is, the story is in itself already a form of interpretation—or, more precisely, the way in which the story is told already contains an interpretation (to an extent, this is also true of a story told in conversation, but much less so). Hence it is important for me to take this implied interpretation apart, to subject it to critical analysis, in terms of my own *sociological* relevance structure.

There is yet another case of interpretation that can only be briefly mentioned here: the interpretation of altogether anonymous structures, regardless of how their meanings are conveyed. This is the problem of interpreting, not the meanings of individuals or groups of individuals (even such as may constitute a specific concrete subculture), but of large institutional constellations. Examples of this would be "the American family," or "the American state," or "the capitalist economy," or "Islamic law." While, of course, every one of these abstractions is represented by concrete human beings engaged in concrete actions, institutions can never be empirically available as such. This, though, by no means implies that institutions are meaningless entities. On the contrary, every human institution is, as it were, a sedimentation of meanings, or, to vary the image, a crystallization of meanings in objective forms. As meanings become objectivated, *institutionalized,* in this manner, they become common reference points for the meaningful actions of countless individuals, even from one generation to another. But these institutionalized meanings can also be interpreted—"retrieved," or "unwrapped," from their seemingly inert forms. The way in which *this* can be done, however, cannot be pursued here.

Instead, we may now turn to the other kind of meaning mentioned earlier—that is, one that is completely outside one's own life-world. Of course, in the example described at some length before the interpreting individual is indeed faced with an unfamiliar, surprising social situation, and the subculture adumbrated in that situation is one in which she has not previously participated. All the same, both the situation and the subculture were not completely unknown to her. As was indicated, she actually had ready-made interpretative schemas "at hand" to begin dealing with the unfamiliar social reality—as witness the ready-made typifications (or, if one prefers, stereotypes) of the Californian way of life. And, after all, the initial informant was an individual with whom conversation was possible in the first place, with whom large chunks of one's own social reality were already shared (as evidenced by the preceding conversation topic of the professional job market), and (last not least) with whom one could converse in standard English. If we had spun out further a variation of the example just alluded to before—about people engaged in some homicidal sacrificial ritual in the midst of an American convention hotel—the process of interpretation, needless to say, would have been different and much more difficult. But, obviously, the best example for the kind of interpretation at issue now is that of a visitor to a more or less completely foreign society:

Let us posit, then, that I am an anthropologist, finally doing fieldwork in one of the few truly untouched jungle spots left in the world (I'm a *lucky* anthropologist). My indigenous informants, across formidable linguistic barriers, are explaining one of *their* homicidal rituals to me (why not?)—say, throwing virgins into the volcano in order to assuage the rain god. Once again, when my efforts at interpretation of this quaint custom are compared with interpretations going on in ordinary situations in my home society, there are both similarities and differences.

As a fully socialized adult engaged in face-to-face interaction with other human beings there is always one possibility open to me (in this case, let us assume, I'm *not* a virgin myself and thus not eligible for fuller participation in the events in question): this is the possibility of "going native." What happens in that event is a process of resocialization, at the end of which I become a member of the meaning system I originally studied as an outsider. Such resocialization is a standing professional hazard for all anthropologists; some of them, of course, may welcome rather than try to avoid this outcome. Be this as it may, the anthropologist who "goes native" has now developed a new "natural attitude" in the originally alien situation. The problems of interpretation are then no different from the ones discussed before within one's own society. The interpreter will share an essentially common relevance structure and body of knowledge with the people whose actions are to be interpreted: "Who are these girls?"—"Going into the volcano"—"Ah yes, of course, it's that time of the year again. How many are there?" . . .

The more interesting case, though, is that of the anthropologist (or, for that matter, any outsider) who does *not* "go native" completely. That is my case, let us assume. I remain what I was before I arrived in the jungle (or so I think), and I seek to interpret the "native" meanings. Any outsider, even a casual tourist, will be constrained to make this effort, but, being an anthropologist, my own attempts are more systematic and self-conscious. Here, of course, everything said before about sociological as against ordinary interpretation will apply, *mutatis mutandis:* there is an anthropological body of theory and data, an anthropological relevance structure and so on. Needless to say, the process of *listening* here is more difficult: I barely understand the language, I fail to observe all sorts of relevant cues in people's statements and actions, there are large areas that completely mystify me—and, let us also assume, the prospect of watching these individuals being thrown into a volcano is at least mildly upsetting to me, so that I have some difficulty maintaining the necessary attitude of calm detachment, of not "interrupting" with my own emotional reactions and moral judgments. To use the familiar anthropological term, I'm likely to suffer from acute culture shock. It is important to point out, though, that such culture shock has some useful side effects. It *forces* me to be fully attentive to everything that is going on, precisely because it is all so shockingly unfamiliar. By contrast, much in my own society ongoingly escapes my attention because it takes place within a structure of familiarity. It may be true that familiarity breeds contempt; more relevantly for the interpreting social scientist, familiarity breeds inattention. The very alienness of the situation, then, is both a difficulty and an asset, cognitively speaking.

If I am to be successful in this situation as an anthropologist—which means *neither* remaining the incomprehending outsider *nor* "going native"—I must, in a very real sense, become a "plural person" (to an extent everyone is that up to a point, especially in a modern pluralistic society, but there is a qualitative jump here). That is, I am both inside and outside the situation, and my activity as a social-scientific interpreter ensures that I maintain this always tenuous balance. The anthropological field researcher is trained to achieve this curious trick, by a variety of techniques; for instance, the practice of keeping continuous field notes, beyond its obvious instrumental utility, is a ritual for maintaining the insider/outsider status. The details of this cannot concern us here. The further point to be made, though, is that the sociologist, even in her or his own society, resembles the anthropologist in this status, despite the fact that the latter is easier to maintain "at home" than in the jungle. One may say that the alienness, which is automatically given to the anthropologist, must be artificially constructed by the sociologist if the perils of inattention to the familiar are to be avoided. Put differently, the anthropologist has the problem of "going native"; the sociologist must strive to "go alien." Put differently again, any act of sociological interpretation introduces an artificial distance, or a strangeness, between interpreter and interpreted.

Increasingly, of course, it is not only anthropologists who study exotic cultures; sociologists have undertaken their own share of such studies. To that degree, the methodological differences between the two disciplines have diminished. But there is yet another point to be made in the matter of interpreting a very alien society. Two distinct cognitive goals are possible. One, I may simply want to *present* this society—as it were, for exhibition in an ethnographic museum. Or, two, I'm interested in *comparing* this society with my own society and with other societies, for the purpose of testing some broad hypotheses or theories. Within the discipline of anthropology there have long been debates as to the respective validity of these two approaches. Within sociology, by contrast, there has never been much debate. Sociology, by its very nature, is comparative and generalizing, and this cognitive goal will dictate the character of the questions to which answers will be sought. Max Weber's vast work in the cross-cultural sociology of religion is the prime example of this comparative and generalizing thrust, though by no means the only example.

Different again, of course, is the interpretation of *past* societies—say, the interpretation of sexual mores or religious practices in ancient Rome. There is much similarity in this to the problems of interpreting a greatly alien society in the present—the barriers of language and lack of information, and the consequent difficulties in grasping the relevance structures in operation. But there are also differences: the sources are much more limited, for one. In the aforementioned jungle society, even if it is illiterate, every living member of that society is a "text" open to interpretation; in the case of ancient Rome, the interpreter is limited to a more or less fixed quantity of written sources, augmented by archaeological evidence. (In that respect, of course, there is the more fortunate case of an interpreter of a society on which a lot of new archaeological discoveries are in process of being made.) Also, in a more radical sense than previously stated with regard to reading a newspaper story, the interpreter cannot ask any questions. There are no living survivors of the society to answer. This further implies that the meanings to be interpreted are "frozen"; they will never change again. By contrast, even in a "primitive" jungle society, meanings always change, are in some sort of flux, as long as there are living human beings who orient their existence by these meanings. One may also say that this "frozen" quality of the past gives it its awesomeness: there are no more Romans, and what they have done and meant is caught in an eternal tableau that will never move again; ancient Rome, unlike any living society, is a "once and for all" reality.

As in the case of anthropology, the interpreter of the past, notably the historian, may have two different cognitive goals: to interpret this past society for its own sake; and to interpret it in order to explain certain features of the present, or of other societies than this particular one. Once more, these are the goals of "ethnography" as against comparison and generalization. Indeed, ever since Edward Gibbon if not earlier, one of the foremost motives attracting scholars to the history of ancient Rome has been the expectation that the latter will furnish "lessons" for the present. And as in anthropology, historians have quarreled over this kind of interest, some sharing it, others arguing that every historical constellation is unique and should be studied for its own sake without pedagogical hindthoughts. The sociologist, whatever the historian may decide to do, will always be inclined to draw lessons from the past—

not, of course, moral or philosophical lessons, but lessons in the sense of finding in the past evidence for this or that generalizing hypothesis about the way societies work. Again, Max Weber is the prime example of such sociological uses of the past.

It may be useful now to sum up the entire discussion of this chapter up to now: In *all* the cases discussed, even in the case of ordinary conversation in everyday life, what is involved is an interpretation of the meanings of others through a complex interaction and interpenetration of relevance structures, meaning systems and bodies of knowledge. What I, the interpreter, find interesting comes up against the others' interests; what I mean and believe to know must, as it were, struggle against their intentions and definitions of reality. If I am not an ordinary observer but a sociologist, the process of interpretation is different in that I am, or should be, much more aware of the dynamics of this interaction, and therefore more in control of it. Also, *qua* sociologist, I am subject to explicit and implicit rules as to how to proceed—the "rules of the game" of the discipline of sociology. Finally, I will then bring into the situation specific *scientific* relevance structures and bodies of knowledge, which are different from those of ordinary persons.

What must be done now is to further clarify the character of this specifically sociological (or, generally, social-scientific) form of interpretation. Put differently, we must further clarify the "rules of the game" of sociology. This can be done conveniently by focusing on a number of key methodological issues.

The issue of conceptualization. There are no "raw facts" in science; there are only facts within a specific conceptual framework. It is important to see, though, that this can also be said of ordinary life. There too, there are no "raw facts," but facts embodied in structures of relevance and meaning. That is, ordinary life is also organized in the minds of all who participate in it, and this organization takes place by means of a conceptual framework—however unsophisticated or illogical this may be, and however dimly the participants may be aware of it. Thus, to go back to an earlier example, the individual (that is, the ordinary individual, not the observing social scientist) who says, "This is an orgy!" may indeed say this on the basis of observing "facts" of an indubitably empirical sort—say, by observing ten people, stark naked, engaging in patently sexual activities on the carpet of this hotel room. But (no pun intended) this "fact" is not "raw" either. It only becomes an observed fact in the first place because the observer is *attentive to it:* after all, our somewhat innocent pedagogue from the provinces might, just conceivably, pay no attention to the naked people on the floor, but instead have her gaze riveted with passionate intensity on the artistic productions hanging on the wall (she is, let us imagine, a connoisseuse of hotel art). Or, alternatively, she might blindly rush into the bathroom and inspect the plumbing, because she is, for whatever intellectual reasons, interested in the latest innovations in that area of modern technology. In other words, her interest in the sexual "facts" in the situation is the result of what psychologists like to call "selective perception" —that is, she perceives *these* particular facts because she is interested in them as against *other* facts that, at least for the moment, she is inattentive to. This interest presupposes a conceptual framework by which the continuous mass of data assaulting the senses is ordered. And, of course, the seemingly spontaneous designation of these particular perceived facts as "an orgy" is the direct application of a *concept* to what is being perceived. That concept presupposes a larger system of concepts relevant to the area of sexual activity. So that, to vary the example, if upon entering the hotel room our observer would have found just two naked individuals, one male and one female, lying on the bed rather than the floor, engaged in sexual activity—whatever she might have called *that* scene, it would hardly have been "an orgy." In that case, within the same overall conceptual framework of sexual activity, *another* concept would have seemed to be more applicable.

But these are not concepts in the strict scientific sense, because they are not sharply defined, their relations to each other are not clarified and their empirical validity is not rigorously tested by evidence—all characteristics of concepts within a scientific frame of reference. The quasi-concepts of ordinary life have an eminently pragmatic purpose—to provide a "map for living." These same quasi-concepts, pragmatically applied in everyday life, are what Alfred Schutz called *typifications,* and, as he amply demonstrated, ordinary social life would be impossible without them: people would not know "what is what."

Now, the sociologist cannot simply adopt the typifications as they are, but she or he must *take cognizance* of them. If this cognizance is missing, no interpretation of what is actually going on may occur. Back to the example: the observer, by saying "This is an orgy!" is applying a concept that, minimally, implies a collective breach of conventional sexual mores. But if she is going to stick by this conceptualization as her inquiry proceeds, it is essential that she take cognizance of what the *actors* in this scene mean by their activity. In other words, in some fashion (not necessarily using the same word) the actors too must be saying to themselves "We are staging an orgy!" If this is *not* what they are saying to themselves, the sociologist's designation of the scene as "an orgy" is doubtful. This can be seen most easily by imagining alternate meaning structures in this situation: suppose that, upon further investigation, it turns out that this hotel room is occupied by an Arabian potentate and his nine concubines, and what they are doing is their normal siesta routine. Or suppose that no real sexual activity is going on at all, but rather a rehearsal of an amateur theatrical group for a spoof of contemporary sex movies. Or that the first perception of the situation was altogether in error: these people are wearing flesh-colored leotards and are practicing for a highly decorous modern dance performance.

What follows from this consideration is simple but of great methodological importance: sociological concepts cannot be models of thought imposed from without (as positivists of all descriptions are wont to do), but rather must relate to the typifications that are already operative in the situation being studied. All human situations carry meaning—if one prefers, are illuminated by meaning from within themselves. The purpose of sociological interpretation is to "bring out" these meanings more clearly, and to relate them (causally and otherwise) to other meanings and meaning systems. Using Schutzian language, sociological concepts are second-order constructs (the first-order constructs, of course, being the typifications that the sociologist already finds within the situation). Or, using Weberian language, sociological concepts must be meaning-adequate (*sinnadaequat*)—that is, they must retain an intelligible connection with the meaningful intentions of the actors in the situation.

This understanding of the nature of social-scientific concepts was developed in great detail in Weber's theory of *ideal types*. All concepts in sociology are "ideal types." Their construction entails a peculiar *translation* of ordinary typifications into the scientific frame of reference. Therefore, they are not "real"—not "really out there"—but are "artificially" constructed for specific cognitive purposes. Take as an example two of Weber's own conceptual creations: *bureaucracy* and *inner-worldly asceticism*. Both are ideal types, in that they were carefully constructed by Weber for purposes of interpretation; neither is nor was "really out there" in the manner defined by Weber. There is a difference between them, though. There have been many individuals in modern societies who would readily say to themselves and to others, "I am a member of a bureaucracy." By contrast, no Puritan entrepreneur ever said to himself, "I am an inner-worldly ascetic." Thus the second concept is at a greater distance from the typifications of the "real" social world than the first. Yet both concepts are "meaning-adequate." A bureaucrat can readily recognize himself in Weber's construction of bureaucracy. And a Puritan entrepreneur, transported by time machine from colonial New England into Weber's Heidelberg study, would certainly have been puzzled by the *term* "inner-worldly asceticism," but, again, he would have had little difficulty recognizing his own moral world in Weber's delineation of it. The difference between the two concepts, and in their respective distance from the typifications of ordinary life, is due to a difference in Weber's cognitive purpose in the two cases. In his analysis of bureaucracy Weber was concerned with a phenomenon specific to the modern world; but the concept of inner-worldly asceticism was constructed in order to undertake comparisons and generalizations of moral systems ranging from ancient India to twentieth-century America, and consequently a more "distanced" concept *had* to be constructed.

It further follows that all sociological concepts have

an *ad hoc* quality. They are constructed for a specific cognitive purpose, and they might be discarded for other purposes. Also, the empirical evidence "out there" may force their abandonment or modification. Thus, if the human beings to whom a concept is applied can *not* "recognize themselves" in it—in the case of living persons, by protesting verbally through their own definitions of their situation; in the case of people in the past, by what could be called "protesting texts" —then the sociologist will be constrained to construct new concepts that will be more adequate to the situation in question.

What has been done in all of this is that the meanings of ordinary life have been transposed into a *different* world of meanings, namely that of the social scientist. This transposition is at the core of sociological interpretation. It also constitutes an incipient *explanation* of the situation in question: the sociological interpreter now not only understands something, but understands it in a new way that was not possible before the transposition took place.

The issue of the outcome of conceptualization. Sociology from its beginnings has been haunted by the positivist ideal. This calls for the establishment of universal laws, in the fashion of the natural sciences, allowing for a system of causally connected relationships under which specific phenomena can be subsumed. If these laws are empirically valid, then the specific phenomena can be deduced from them as cases and predictions can be made as to their future course.

The previous description of conceptualization shows the weakness of this ideal. Social phenomena will inevitably be distorted if their inherent meanings are ignored. But this insight has further implications: laws are supposed to have universal validity; human meaning systems do not.

Take by way of example a sociologist's attempt to interpret political actions, undertaken by a particular group in a particular situation. Suppose that this interpretation is to follow a putative law that people vote in order to maximilize their own interests. This, of course, is not altogether false. But what people consider to be their own interests depends on their meaning systems—and these can *not* be deduced from the aforementioned law. For example, an observer may conclude that candidate X in a particular election clearly represents the interests of the majority of the voters in the district—in terms, say, of the economic policies being proposed by this candidate. But it so happens that the voters are not primarily concerned with economic issues. Rather, their attention is focused on ethnicity—and a large number of them have defined as their primary interest the election of candidates belonging to their own ethnic group, an affiliation that candidate X lacks. In other words, the interests in the situation are not the interests posited by the observer. The observer may well believe that these people's definition of the situation is irrational, even morally reprehensible, but this belief will be of no help whatever in interpreting this situation (and, not so incidentally, in predicting the outcome of the election).

Conceptualization as here understood can indeed assist in the establishment of causal connections ("candidate X lost the election because he is not Italian"), but only if the meanings operative in the situation are taken into account. The same, of course, goes for prediction.

Somewhat different from positivism is the functionalist ideal. This calls for the discovery of functions independent of what the actors in a social situation intend (the "latent functions" of Robert Merton; to discover the "manifest functions," of course, no great sociological explorations are needed, at least not in one's own society). Back to another earlier example: the underlying function of the sacrificial ritual around the volcano is not to ensure continuing rain but rather to serve the economic interests of the priesthood—say, because the ceremonies require expensive equipment, which is monopolistically produced and rented out for the occasion by the priestly caste.

Once again, this type of explanation is not to be rejected out of hand. But a distinction will have to be made (based, of course, on the empirical evidence). One possibility is that the priests are fully aware of these economic ramifications, indeed that this is why they or their predecessors invented the ritual in the first place. In that case, the economic interest is not a "latent function" at all—not for the priests, that is—but the manifest meaning of what they are doing. The other possibility (not at all uncommon) is that the priests—along with the general populace and (who knows?) perhaps even the about-to-be-sacrificed virgins—sincerely believe that the sole purpose of the operation is to induce the rain god to continue making rain. That is, the priests themselves (like so many sincere people) are not aware of their economic interests, do not define such interests as motives either to themselves or to others, and would violently resent it if such motives were imputed to them. In that case, the sociologist may well use a term such as "latent function." Or, using Weberian language, the sociologist may say that the economic benefits are "unintended consequences" of these actions. Both usages are acceptable, as long as it is clear that this is an explanation in the mind of the scientific observer only and is not imputed in any way to the social reality "out there." This should be even clearer if, in the tradition of Emile Durkheim and

Anglo-American functionalism, the "latent function" of the ritual is explained in terms of the maintenance of collective solidarity (an explanation in which all the specifics of the ritual turn out to be incidental). In all cases of explanation in terms of "latency," the actors, of course, will not recognize themselves in the explanation—which is acceptable, just as long as such self-recognition is not imputed to them on some empirically unavailable level. (The question as to whether there might be "unconscious motives," in the psychoanalytic sense, cannot be pursued here.)

The issue of evidence. Evidence in sociology must always be framed in terms of meaning. More precisely, the second-order constructs of the scientific observer must be ongoingly related to the first-order constructs of ordinary life. Consequently, the falsification of the sociologist's hypotheses must also be framed in terms of meaning.

Back to the example of the election campaign: I (the sociologist analyzing the campaign) am interested in the chances of candidate X. In order to explore any hypothesis I may have in the matter, I must seek to understand the meanings in play in this particular district. Thus I have hypothesized that candidate X will win, because he represents the economic interests of the North End. But now I have gone out and discovered that most of the voters in the North End do not define their political interests in economic terms at all. My hypothesis is falsified precisely because it did not take cognizance of the meanings operative in the situation. I now modify it, and say, "Although candidate X represents the economic interests of the North End better than either of his two opponents, he will lose because he is Irish." Needless to say, that is still a hypothesis and not a statement of apodictic truth, and the prediction may turn out to be false on election day (thus it may happen that, as they enter the voting booth, a lot of these Italians suddenly remember their economic interests and bracket their ethnic enthusiasms and antagonisms for the next three minutes). That is, any social-scientific hypothesis is a statement of *probabilities*. (My hypothesis, incidentally, will remain probabilistic even after election day: I definitely know now that candidate X has lost the election; I can still only hypothesize *why* he lost.)

Sociological interpretation is not a philosophical enterprise. It is always subject to testing by empirical evidence. Sociological propositions are never axioms, but empirically falsifiable hypotheses. In that they are similar to propositions in all sciences. But evidence and falsification in sociology are not the same as in the natural sciences—precisely because they always involve meanings.

There is the further question as to the manner in which the evidence is gathered—in the parlance of American sociology, the question of *methods* (as against the question of *method,* in the sense of a general intellectual approach). For a long time this question has been posed in terms of qualitative versus quantitative methods. It is unfortunate that the understanding of sociological interpretation being presented here has often been coupled with an antagonism toward quantitative methods. That is a misunderstanding. *Nothing whatsoever in the present statement should be construed as implying a preference for qualitative over quantitative methods of empirical research.* There is nothing wrong whatever with quantitative methods—*as long as* they are used to clarify the meanings operative in the situation being studied. The choice between the two kinds of methods should, at least ideally, be based on nothing but their respective chances of obtaining the evidence being sought. (We know that, in a less than ideal world, there are also considerations of available resources and skills, but these are not considerations of methodological principle.) Thus, in the example, the decision may be made that, in order to delve into the minds of North End voters, an elaborate survey may be necessary—with the most rigorously designed and pretested questionnaire, its administration to a stratified sample of the voting population and the application of the most sophisticated statistical techniques to the ensuing data (including the use of the latest computer hardware). On the other hand, it may be decided that two or three thoroughly trained researchers hanging around the bars, stores and church halls of the North End may be quite enough to obtain the desired information. The decision will depend on cognitive as well as practical considerations, about which one cannot generalize. The point to be made here is that *either* the quantitative *or* the qualitative option may fully satisfy the sociological "rules of the game" in the acquisition of evidence.

The issue of objectivity. Interpretation, as proposed so far, has been understood by some critics of a positivistic persuasion as implying "pure subjectivism," "intuition" or "empathy"—that is, as an attempt to acquire knowledge without controls or correctives. Perhaps enough has been said already to show that this is a misunderstanding and that interpretation is not a guessing game where anything goes. The issue here, of course, is that of the objectivity of sociological interpretation, and the character of this objectivity needs to be spelled out a little further—and not only against positivistic critics who want to introduce criteria of objectivity derived from the natural sciences, but also against critics of altogether different persuasion, who deny that objectivity of any sort is possible in the interpretation of social reality.

The social location, the psychological constitution and the cognitive peculiarities of an interpreter are inevitably involved in the act of interpretation, and all of them will affect the interpretation. Thus, as I interpret the orgiastic goings-on in that hotel, I must reckon with certain facts—such as that I am an upwardly mobile middle-class Protestant Midwesterner, that I am a woman in my late twenties just emerged from a painful love affair that has made me suspicious of academic men, that I will avoid statistical methods if at all possible because I can't add, and that I have a consuming desire to disprove the Schulze-Merriwether hypothesis on sexual deviance (Schulze is a former roommate of mine and I hate her guts). Now, it would clearly be foolish to assert that all such factors can always be controlled by the conscientious sociologist, and that objectivity means that factors of this kind have been antiseptically removed from the interpretative enterprise. That, however, is not the point.

Rather, the point is that the sociologist can control these factors, certainly in principle and to a large degree in fact, by adhering to the previously discussed rules of scientific relevance structure and evidence. The scientific relevance structure first of all means that I can tell myself, "I am now doing sociology"—and *ipso facto* am *not* expressing my petty-bourgeois morality, my resentments against *homo academicus,* or my wish to prove Schulze wrong. But much more is involved than a pious intention to be objective if I can. The scientific relevance structure brings with it a body of empirical knowledge that must be taken into account in any specific interpretation. The same relevance structure provides the context of any concepts generated by the interpreter. These concepts must have explanatory uses, bringing the new to-be-interpreted phenomena into a meaningful relation with comparable phenomena previously interpreted by other sociologists. This relation does not spring arbitrarily from the interpreter's subjectivity. It rests on a generally available body of theory and data, and it must be ongoingly established in interaction with new empirical evidence. The empirical data, my own and those of others, always "have their say," although they "speak" within the conceptual scheme that I (and others) have constructed. Objectivity, then, does *not* mean that the sociologist reports on "raw facts" that are "out there" in and of themselves. Rather, objectivity means that the sociologist's conceptual scheme is in a dialectical relationship with the empirical data.

The classical case of Max Weber's work on "inner-worldly asceticism" may once more be cited. Various biographers have tried to illuminate Weber's social, psychological and other extrascientific "interests" in the question of the relationship of religious morality to the origins of modern capitalism. Yet the concept and the vast assemblage of hypotheses it has generated have been used and continue to be used by social scientists and historians who share none of Weber's extrascientific concerns. And the question of whether the famous "Protestant ethic thesis" is or is not objectively valid as an interpretation of certain facets of modern history cannot be decided as a result of any amount of delving into Weber's biography or psyche.

Put differently, *scientific objectivity is a specific relevance structure into which an individual can shift in his or her consciousness*. Those who deny that such a shift is possible must also deny the *general* possibility of shifts of relevance within consciousness—but such a denial would be in palpable contradiction to ordinary experience as well as scientific evidence. Thus we know

that such shifts do in fact occur all the time even in ordinary life. Sexuality once again may serve as a very
clear example: I am talking about a matter of shared
political interest with an individual of the opposite sex.
As the conversation proceeds, I become aware of a
strong, possibly mutual physical attraction. From that
point on the relevance structure of the conversation
shifts drastically, and what began as, say, a campaign
planning session is transformed into a seduction strategy. Or, conversely, I may be engaged in a highly
erotic exchange when the other individual voices a
political opinion that I find highly objectionable. Since
I am a person who is very *engagé* politically, I find it
impossible to continue my erotic focus in the face of
this suddenly revealed political disagreement. I begin
to argue politically, and I as I do this (no wonder) I
lose the sensation of physical attraction (at least tem-
porarily). In other words, in ordinary life sexuality
provides a relevance structure *into which* and *out of
which* I can move with considerable ease. One may
add that, unless I am either a sex maniac or (in the
aforementioned example) a political fanatic, I can
control these movements to a considerable extent.

This is true *a fortiori* of the scientific relevance
structure. It is characterized by a much higher degree
of awareness and controls, which can be learned and internalized by the scientific interpreter. Indeed, just this
is one of the most important things one should learn in
the course of sociological training. But also, very importantly, this specific relevance structure is *institutionalized*. This happens in what Charles Peirce called
the *community of investigators*. In the case of the sociologist, there is the community of sociologists, both living and dead, who are "present" in consciousness as a
sort of scientific "generalized other." In slightly
different language, the community of sociologists, "the

discipline," provides a "reference group" with which every individual sociologist ongoingly interacts, both externally by means of social relations, but also within the mind. Objectivity, not just as an ideal but ever again as an experienced reality, is the result of this ongoing interaction between the individual sociologist and the community of sociologists. By the very nature of scientific activity, the body of objective knowledge thus accumulated is never finally fixed, is always tentative and subject to revision, even revision made necessary by the uncovering of extrascientific interests. None of this revisionist activity, however, negates the methodological principle of objectivity. On the contrary, it bears witness to its perduring validity—for, if science did not strive for objectivity, no revisions would be necessary in the first place.

The objectivity of sociological interpretation is closely related to what Max Weber called *value-freeness*—a concept that has been endlessly and often confusedly debated. We know that in ordinary life people's interpretations are bound by their values. In principle, this is also true of sociologists. They are, after all, members of society and participate in its values. Clearly, in many cases these values will provide the motives by which a sociologist became interested in a particular phenomenon to begin with. Thus, for example, it is quite clear that many if not most American sociologists who studied phenomena of race did so because the racial patterns of American society offended their values. Not only is it not wrong that such motives affect the work of sociologists, but it is inevitable. That is not the point. Rather, the point is that once these sociologists embark on their scientific inquiry, they must "bracket" these values as much as possible—not, needless to say, in the sense of giving them up or trying to forget them, but in the sense of controlling the way in which these values might distort the sociological vision. If such bracketing is not done, the scientific enterprise collapses, and what the sociologist then believes to perceive is nothing but a mirror image of his own hopes and fears, wishes, resentments or other psychic needs; what he will then *not* perceive is anything that can reasonably be called social reality.

This bracketing cannot be guaranteed by rigorous research methods. These can be influenced by values as much as less rigorous methods—even resentments can be quantified! Value-freeness is a cognitive act of a different order. In a way, it is an ascetic ideal—a certain asceticism of the mind—and it is often hard to achieve, especially of course in cases where one's own values are strongly engaged. It is above all a *passion to see,* to see clearly, regardless of one's likes or dislikes, hopes or fears. The bracketing of one's own values implies a systematic openness to the values of others as they are relevant to the situation being studied—even if these values are quite repugnant to oneself: seeing is not approving, but I cannot see at all if I constantly voice my own disapproval.

To strive for objectivity and value-freeness is to erect a crucial safeguard against dogmatism in science. A useful rule for doing this is the one suggested by Karl Popper—the constant and systematic search for falsifying data: that is, when I propose a hypothesis—precisely because I know that there may be values of mine that are relevant to the proposition—the most important thing that I must do is to search for those data that may falsify rather than support my hypothesis. Summing up on this issue: we agree with the positivists that there is such a thing as scientific objectivity (even if in practice it is often difficult to achieve). We disagree with the positivists in insisting that the objectivity of an interpretative science cannot be the same as the objectivity of the natural sciences. As to the critics of sociological objectivity from the other side, radical antipositivists who deny the possibility of any separation of values from scientific inquiry (such as is common today among various people who would like to ideologize sociology and turn it into an instrument of advocacy), we agree with them that extrascientific interests often interfere with the act of interpretation, as we also agree that such interferences ought to be uncovered. We disagree that these facts negate either the principle or the practical possibility of an objective social science. Further aspects of this position of ours will be taken up again in the next chapter.

The issue of applicability. Almost all knowledge about society can be applied by somebody in the service of this or that pragmatic project. This is unavoidable. But it is all the more important to understand the following: sociological interpretation is the result of a very specific cognitive process, within the specific relevance structure outlined above. As soon as the contents of this interpretation are to be applied to *action* in society, this relevance structure is abandoned. All action presupposes an altogether different relevance structure. Among other things, what must be abandoned now is the bracketing of one's own values. All application is necessarily value-based. Thus, for example, I can write a sociological treatise detailing, say, the patterns of race relations in a particular American community while bracketing my own racial values—which, let us assume, are liberal and therefore in tension with various illiberal features of the *status quo*. Suppose that my inquiry has produced further knowledge of the situation. It is inconceivable that this knowledge can be applied to action without reference to my values; indeed, the likelihood is that I will now act in order to maximize the realization of my liberal values in this particular situation. But it also follows that there is no way by which "what ought to be done" can be directly deduced from my previous sociological interpretation. Thus I may have discovered in my study that there is a specific income gap as between comparable groups of whites and blacks in this community, and my value position leads me to deplore this finding. But, as I want to move now from interpretation to action, a number of possible courses of action are open to me—legal action to enforce nondiscrimination laws or affirmative action guidelines, unionization, special training and retraining programs, encouraging black business enterprise, and yet others. My choice among these various possibilities will be affected by considerations of values as well as practical feasibility assessments, and my choice will of course *also* be affected by various other items of sociological knowledge. But it will not be possible for me to say, to myself or to others, "This is what I have found; *therefore,* this is what ought to be done."

One of the abuses of sociology has been the ignoring of this indirect relation between understanding and action, of the shift in relevance structure necessitated by the movement from the first to the second. It is in consequence of this confusion that sociological concepts or findings are then used as *legitimations* of courses of action that are based on particular values. That is, sociology has been used to hide the value-presuppositions of this or that course of action. For example, it is one thing to state that a majority of both whites and blacks disapprove, say, of interracial marriage, quite another thing to say that *therefore* there ought to be laws forbidding interracial marriage—or, on the contrary, that *therefore* there ought to be educational programs to promote them.

A methodological and a moral imperative come together here in certain requirements by which sociologists ought to abide: One, that it be made clear that sociological knowledge is of a peculiar kind, deriving from a specific scientific frame of reference that is *different* from the frame of reference of the man in the street, the political activist or anyone else. (This is not just an individual matter, but a concern of the vocation of sociologist as a profession.) Two, that sociologists cannot make recommendations except in an "if . . . then" form, which is itself an interpretative process— *"If* you want to achieve goal *x, then* these findings of mine are relevant to your choice of possible actions." Three, no normative implications can be directly drawn from sociological concepts or findings; in other words, the sociologist cannot be a moral guide.

It goes without saying that, lengthy though this chapter is, it has not exhausted the ramifications of what is involved in the act of sociological interpretation. One final point, though: interpretation, as described here, may be found in different schools of sociology—including various groupings of Marxists, Durkheimians and structural functionalists. Sociological interpretation, in other words, is not a "sectarian" property. Nevertheless, as has been made amply clear, we believe that the Weberian tradition offers the most satisfactory approach to this matter, as it also evinces the most sophisticated awareness of the precarious relations between understanding and values on the one hand, and of understanding and responsible action on the other.

3

SOCIOLOGICAL INTERPRETATION AND THE PROBLEM OF RELATIVITY

In the first chapter we discussed the origins of the sociological perspective in a shock experience—to wit, the experience of suddenly perceiving the dynamics of hitherto unperceived forces underneath the "official" façades of the social order. This experience was, and continues to be, relativizing in itself: the world is not what it appears and pretends to be, and therefore all statements about the world cannot be taken seriously in an earlier attitude of "innocence." And in the preceding chapter we compared the sociological perspective with the "culture shock" undergone by a visitor to an alien society—with the important difference that most sociologists undergo this shock while remaining physically within their own society. All forms of culture shock are also *ipso facto* relativizing. Indeed, at the core of the shock is the insight that perceptions and norms previously taken for granted are now revealed to be highly relative in terms of space and time. In Pascal's famous words, what is truth on one side of the Pyrenees is error on the other; the implication is that our own notions of truth and error are dependent on our location in geography and history, and thus dependent on the accident of birth.

Thus relativity was, from the beginning, an object of study of the discipline of sociology. If Frenchmen believe in value A and Spaniards in a contradictory value B, sociologists have always been interested in exploring further to what extent this difference can be explained in terms of various characteristics of these two societies (and, needless to say, the same interest pertains to differences within a society, say between classes, or ethnic groups, or regions). Yet it would be a one-sided view to see sociology simply as a discipline (one among several) interested in the study of relativity. Sociology is also a *product* of the same relativity that has always been one of its objects of study. Put graphically, if relativity were understood as a disease, then the diagnosis would itself be part and parcel of the pathological syndrome.

It should not be difficult to see why this is so. Unless the sociologist has himself undergone the shock of relativity, the very phenomenon of relativity would not have entered his awareness. One could presumably imagine a situation where this would not be so. An individual possessed of absolute certainty with regard to his own perceptions and values could, theoretically, be interested in studying the empirically available fact that there are other people not sharing these perceptions and values. This individual would then proceed to seek explanations as to why these other people are so blind to what to him are obvious truths, and these explanations could well take a sociological form (such as the form of class analysis). The trouble with this theoretical possibility is that, once such sociological explanations are undertaken, they are "infectious"—that is, it becomes very difficult to exempt oneself from the explanations made of the positions of others. Be this as it may theoretically, in the actual history of the discipline the experience of relativity and the study of relativity have gone hand in hand. It is clear that this linkage poses a serious methodological problem for sociology. Put graphically again, it is somewhat akin to the problem of how one is to push a car in which one is riding.

It is important to see that sociology is but one of the manifestations of the deepening sense of relativity in modern Western history, otherwise one either blames it too much or gives it more credit than is due. Albert Salomon has explored the roots of sociology in this broad historical development. In a different manner, Arnold Gehlen has been concerned with the relationship of sociological perspective to what he called the "subjectivization" of modern Western culture—the process by which what previously was considered to be objective reality came to be understood as the result of subjective choices. In this sense, indeed, the problem of relativity is at the heart of what we know as modern Western culture, understandable as a kind of progressive disintegration of an order of objective certainty embodied in Christendom. On the level of intellectual reflection, the same problem gave birth to the so-called turn to the subjective, at least from Descartes on—a new and radical concern with the structures of human subjectivity, motivated precisely by deepening uncertainty as to what one may call objectively real. More proximately, sociology was part of the same intellectual wave that brought the problem of history to the fore in nineteenth-century European thought. Hegel, Feuerbach, Marx, Nietzsche and Freud were the promulgators of this new historicism, which first dissolved and then tried to reorder the old order of objectivity. It is obviously beyond our present scope to pursue this historical revolution in modern Western thought; it is only mentioned here to situate sociology in a much broader cultural and intellectual context.

What has just been said about the relation of sociology and the problem of relativity applies to the discipline as a whole, not just to this or that segment of it. Thus even the sober survey researcher, with few if any philosophical worries, contributes to the modern crisis of relativity, as he finds, for example, that political opinions vary with income, religious beliefs with occupation, sexual mores with class and so on. But within the development of sociology the problem of relativity has appeared most sharply in the subdiscipline known as the sociology of knowledge.

Again, it cannot be our purpose to give either a historical outline or a systematic presentation of the sociology of knowledge. First given this name in the 1920s by Max Scheler, the sociology of knowledge was brought into English-speaking social science by Karl Mannheim. In American sociology, where it still remains a somewhat marginal subdiscipline, it merged with various other intellectual trends, such as social psychology in the tradition of George Herbert Mead, phenomenology and more recently neo-Marxism. It can be said without too much simplification that the sociology of knowledge is an enormous elaboration of Pascal's insight into the social relativity of human notions of truth. Put differently, the sociology of knowledge understands and studies the *constructed* character of what human beings mean by "reality."

A useful concept in this enterprise is that of *plausibility structure*. Different people find different definitions of reality plausible. Thus, say in the eighteenth century (more so than in Pascal's time), a Spanish husband might have found it plausible to define his wife's infidelity as a slur on his honor to be avenged in blood, while a French husband might have found it more plausible to accept her behavior with tolerance if not good humor. These different norms, however, were clearly not the result of individual ethical conclusions on the part of individual husbands. Rather, the different norms were anchored in specific social contexts—and only in these contexts did the norms remain plausible. The social context for any set of norms or alleged bodies of "knowledge" is the plausibility structure of the latter. As long as a specific plausibility structure prevails in the life of an individual, the appropriate definitions of reality will be plausible to him. If, however, the plausibility structure is changed, it can be predicted that subjective plausibility will change too. Thus the Spanish husband who migrates to France is likely to become less bloody in defense of his putative honor, while the French husband who moves to Spain is likely to develop hitherto undreamed-of codes of honor. The ramifications of this sociological concept of plausibility are very far-reaching, but there is nothing mysterious about the concept. It is undoubtedly rooted in the fundamental constitution of human beings, in the ineradicable sociality of *homo sapiens*. What is more, the plausibility structure of any particular set of reality definitions—be they norms or values, or normatively neutral beliefs about the nature of the world—is eminently accessible to empirical investigation, by the same methods that a sociologist uses to study any other aspect of the social order. Thus it is no more difficult to study—and to interpret—Spanish codes of family honor than any other aspect of Spanish society.

The problem arises as soon as one asks about the relation of *plausibility* and *validity*. The sociologist can objectively describe and explain the plausibility of a particular definition of reality. But, to the extent that this definition of reality pertains to the empirically available social world, the sociologist will also be constrained to ask whether it is valid. This is particularly so with cognitive as against normative definitions of reality. It should be clear by now that the sociologist, *qua* sociologist, is not in a position to arbitrate between Spanish and French family values. But Spaniards and Frenchmen define what *is* socially as well as what they think *ought to be*. And if a Spaniard in the eighteenth century declared, for example, that Spain was economically the most advanced country in Europe because it had the most gold, the sociologist (perhaps after a brief consultation with an economist) could have stated that this belief was wrong. That is, although the Spaniard found this belief *plausible* (a fact that can be explained by analyzing his plausibility structure), this belief could also be declared to be *invalid* by objective methods of social-scientific analysis. But how can the sociologist carry off such a statement? Can the sociology of knowledge not be turned against him too? After all, sociological propositions too, depend on a specific plausibility structure—that of a social context in which the discipline of sociology is accepted. Kidnap the sociologist and imprison him in a Spanish monastery, and it is likely that his erstwhile sociological propositions will soon become implausible in his own mind. Put simply, *if the sociologist too, lives in a world of relativities, is he somehow immune to the cognitive consequences of this fact?* The answer must be *Of course not!* That, however, is the beginning rather than the end of the methodological problem.

The core of the problem is easily stated: how is it possible to reconcile the methodological position proposed in the preceding chapter with the insights of the sociology of knowledge? More specifically: *If science, along with all other cognitive systems, is socially constructed, how can one claim objectivity for it?* If put in this way, the answer is already implied in the discussion of objectivity in the preceding chapter. Of course science is a social construction. Indeed, the character of this construction can, in principle, be analyzed and explained, using the tools of the sociology of knowledge. We have already done this, albeit briefly, in our discussion of the origins of sociology as an intellectual discipline. To use the phrase by Robert Friedrichs, there can be "a sociology of sociology"—perhaps an inspiring case of a physician diagnosing his own malady. But there is a more basic answer: *The possibility of scientific objectivity is grounded in the multiplicity of relevance structures within consciousness.* Each of these relevance structures has particular characteristics, which impose themselves or are submitted to as one "moves into" it in the mind. Science is a particular relevance structure, with particular characteristics —one of which is objectivity, as previously described! To deny the specificity of the scientific relevance structure implies the denial of any possible passage between relevance structures, and implies conversely the assertion that consciousness is always "all of one piece"— that is, that *all* relevances and interests are, at all times and in all places, co-present in the mind. Both the denial and the assertion are flagrantly at odds with the empirical evidence.

For example: I am a Frenchman, just arrived in Madrid on my first visit. Along with a large number of other passengers I emerge from the airport terminal and enter a taxi. Where am I going? (Or, perhaps more accurately, what will be my destination after I have checked into my hotel and gotten myself ready for my first foray into the city?) The answer, very obviously, will depend on the relevance structure that served as the motive for my trip and that will organize my activities while I am here. I may systematically cover all the major tourist attractions, or I might dash to the Prado Museum and spend several days looking at nothing except Velasquez pictures. I might seek out people to converse about the condition of the Catholic Church in Spain—or I might converse with people at random, because I simply want to practice my Spanish. I might spend all my time in discotheques—or gay bars. I might never step outside my hotel, where I'm attending an international convention of stamp collectors (in which case the Madrid location is completely irrelevant to me—the convention could just as well be in Indianapolis). Alternatively, I could devote all my time in Madrid to lessons with a famous guitar teacher, or in business negotiations with somebody just flown in from Saudi Arabia, or in efforts to join the Basque underground (perhaps I'm an explosives expert). And then (almost forgot that one!) I could go out and do sociological research in Madrid—my stay there happens to be part of an international research project on, say, the time budgets of housewives. Note again: as I move within one relevance structure, I shut out of my mind all the other ones that are theoretically possible. I look at pictures by Velasquez, and *not* by Goya; I'm seeking information on religion, and *not* on economic development, and so on. But it is quite possible that I might switch relevance structures in the course of any one of these projects. I stumble into the wrong room at the Prado, and I get so intrigued by Goya that I forget Velasquez; or I fall in love with the nun who is telling me about the condition of the church; or (for the first time in my life) I discover the ecstasies of stamp collecting, abandoning my original project and staying with the convention in my hotel.

Every act of attention implies a corresponding act of inattention. Scientific attentiveness is one case of this. As I am attentive to a phenomenon scientifically, other possible modes of attentiveness are bracketed—such as economic self-interest, erotic excitement, moral passion and so on. In this balancing of attention and inattention, science is no different from other activities of the mind; it differs in the systematic character of both the attention and the inattention, and of course it differs in the specifics that are attended and *not* attended to. To say that this scientific relevance structure is not hermetically sealed off from all other relevance structures is not to make a telling statement against the principle of objectivity, but is simply a general description of how the human mind works.

There have been various forms of radical relativism in modern Western thought, all denying the principle of objectivity not only empirically ("scientists are rarely if ever objective") but theoretically ("there can be no such thing as scientific objectivity"). All varieties of theoretical relativism suffer from the logical flaw of circularity: if all statements about the world are socially determined and therefore not objective, what is the cognitive status of one's own statements? *Including* the statement about the social determination of all knowledge? There have been different escape hatches from this logical dilemma. What they all have in common is the positing of a particular social location that renders one immune, or minimally less susceptible to, the ravages of relativity. The paradigmatic escape hatch is Hegel's: a higher cognitive status attaches to those who are embodiments of the *Zeitgeist*. Marxists of all denominations have attached this privileged status to the proletariat or (if the proletariat turned out to be hard to find—or, worse, refused to have a Marxist consciousness) to this or that self-defined "vanguard of the proletariat." *Mutatis mutandis,* other social collectivities can be identified as a sort of epistemological elite—women, blacks, inhabitants of the

Third World—or, conversely, men, whites or native-born Americans. And the same cognitive crown can be bestowed on yet different groups if the relativism is psychological rather than sociological: only those who have undergone psychoanalysis perceive the world correctly, while everyone else is caught in "rationalizations."

As Karl Mannheim and others have shown, this "containment" of relativity must fail. The same methods of analysis that disclose the relativity of the beliefs of others will, invariably, disclose the relativity of one's own beliefs—if, that is, these methods are consistently applied. The methodological position argued here, though, shows another reason for this failure. There is a sort of hidden positivism in many of the aforementioned forms of radical relativism; that is the expectation that, *if only* one had the correct standpoint, one would then have direct access to facts and laws (such as the "laws of history" or the "laws of the psyche"). As we have tried to show, such direct access is never possible, no matter what one's standpoint. In other words, there is no magical trick by which one can bypass the act of interpretation.

Karl Mannheim found his own escape hatch in the theory of the intelligentsia. Supposedly, there was a group of "freely suspended" intellectuals, who were sufficiently free of vested class interests to be able to attain not an objective, but at least a *more* objective vision of society. Mannheim's theory of the intelligentsia has been pretty effectively demolished. Precisely by using the tools of the sociology of knowledge, one can demonstrate that, far from being "freely suspended," intellectuals constitute a collectivity (some would even say a class) with very specific interests—and, as with other people, these interests color their perceptions of society. Yet Mannheim was not completely wrong. As we have shown, the act of interpretation, if undertaken by the social scientist, posits a community that has been internalized within the consciousness of the individual. This is the community of all the other social scientists, or of all sociologists both living and dead, and this community serves as a very important point of reference (or "reference group") within the mind of the social scientist. This is what Charles Peirce called the community of investigators; or one might employ here a much older term—the "republic of scholars." And that in turn suggests a useful image. By becoming a social scientist, an individual obtains citizenship in this particular republic. But, except for very rare cases (scientific hermits, as it were), he does not thereby renounce his ordinary citizenship in society and in various societal groupings. Consequently, being a social scientist means enjoying (or, if one prefers, suffering from) the peculiar status of *dual citizenship*. And just as some nation-states deny this status to its citizens, so do some human communities deny any rights to the scientist as a citizen of the republic of scholars—for example, the revolutionary movement that demands that the sociologist never, not even for one moment, step outside the relevance structure of its political ideology. Put simply, just as dual citizenship is unacceptable to nationalists, so is objective science intolerable to ideologues.

The act of interpretation necessarily involves a specific detachment. This includes a bracketing of the interpreter's own standpoint. Both the methodology and the institutionalization of a science, such as sociology, is designed to make this bracketing possible—empirically speaking, to give it a reasonable chance. This process of detachment or bracketing has a certain ascetic quality. Yet it is clear that the sociologist will continue to be a member of society, with all the relativizing implications of this. Also, objectivity, as understood here, is a quality of the interpretative process itself, *not* (as positivists would have it) a quality of "the facts out there."

Most broadly speaking, the sociology of knowledge deals with the relation of structures of consciousness and institutional structures. As such it is one aspect of the overall enterprise of interpretative sociology. This aspect is always there, since every social reality contains both consciousness and institutions. But not all sociological interpretation can be done by means of sociology-of-knowledge tools. The basic reason for this is that social actions have unintended consequences that are *not* in the consciousness of the actors and that generate institutional dynamics with a frequently high degree of autonomy (this latter fact, incidentally, is the core of what Marx called alienation—a valid but needlessly pejorative concept). Thus it is not possible to analyze social change using *only* the conceptual instrumentarium of the sociology of knowledge. For example, the frequently autonomous dynamics of economic institutions must be analyzed in terms of that dynamics—generally speaking, this means in terms of the perspective of economics—and not only in terms of the interaction between economic institutions and various contents of consciousness.

The sociology of knowledge, perhaps more than any other aspect of sociology, raises philosophical questions, some of which have just been touched upon. But in itself the sociology of knowledge is not philosophy but rather a part of sociology as an empirical discipline. It therefore falls under the general methodological rules discussed in the preceding chapter, *including* the rules of objectivity. Take, for instance, the concept of ideology. The concept has a long history that cannot be pursued here, but for the present purpose it is enough to say that an ideology is a set of definitions of reality legitimating specific vested interests in society. A sociology-of-knowledge proposition, then, would be, "Belief system X is an ideology, in that it explains and justifies the vested interests of group Y." Such a proposition, assuming that it is empirically grounded in evidence, is an objective and "value-free" statement, despite the fact that the proposition brackets the question as to whether the belief system is finally valid or not.

For example: a particular group—say, college professors—believes itself to be victimized in terms of income. That is, college professors believe that they are underpaid. Typically, such a belief is not merely based on an *ideal* income (thus I, as a college professor, believe that an annual salary of one million dollars, tax-free and with liberal fringe benefits, would be a reasonable remuneration for the services I perform for the common weal), but is also based on some sort of *comparison* with other groups. Thus I believe that I, as a college professor, am underpaid because my income is less than that of, say, business executives, or electricians, or government employees. If my group is organized to defend and foster its collective interests, this comparison will almost certainly be part of the group's public rhetoric. "Is it fair," asks the representative of our union in negotiating with the university for a pay raise, "that full professors at this institution have an average annual salary that is only one half that of senior executives at the so-and-so manufacturing company?" (one of whose senior executives, let us assume, is a member of the board of trustees participating in the negotiations). Leave aside for a moment the question of how to assess fairness as a norm; what is involved in our union negotiator's rhetorical question is not just a normative but a factual statement: the average annual salary of these professors is one half that of these executives. Now, it will not be difficult to argue that this particular proposition of income economics has an ideological function. It justifies the professors' feelings of resentment and their efforts to improve their economic position, and indeed it is right now a weapon in one such effort. If the interpreter of this situation has broader interests, this particular ideological item (a belief about certain economic facts) can eventually be placed in a much wider ideological framework—the beliefs and world view of the American professoriate as a class. Almost certainly, this wider ideological analysis will come upon other items that are not so readily traced to material ambitions. No matter: here is one specific belief, which has a specific ideological function. The interpreter can make this statement *regardless* of whether this income differential is or is not empirically valid. That is, economic analysis may or may not support the belief, but in *either* case the statement about its ideological character can be retained.

Interpreting a definition of reality as ideological, like all interpretations, involves an effort at distancing. And, needless to say, this distancing is more difficult if I am existentially involved in the situation—I'm a professor myself, indeed a professor of economics, and I fervently hope that my economic research will undergird rather than weaken my public position that I'm underpaid. Yet such distancing, even in the midst of battle, is by no means impossible. One could further argue that it is *especially* important in the midst of battle. Military success goes to those who know the terrain and therefore can make the most effective use of it. In this case, if I'm to improve my group's economic position by means of union negotiations, it is best that I know the general economic lay of the land, and that I know it as objectively as possible. In pursuit of my political strategy it may then well be that I keep certain knowledge I have out of my public rhetoric. I might even decide to lie. This raises ethical questions, but not methodological ones.

The concept of objectivity proposed here implies that the sociologist can make statements about the empirical validity or invalidity of people's beliefs about the social world. If so, can the sociologist then go on to say that some people are in "false consciousness"? Not if this phrase is to imply anything beyond the adequacy of empirical information available to these people. Back to the example: here is a group that believes itself to be victimized because of a specific income differential. That is, these professors believe themselves to be victims of society because they are underpaid. Is there any scientific procedure by which this belief could be subsumed under the category of "false consciousness"? The sociologist (in this case presumably employing data collected by economists) can provide data on income distribution among different occupational groups. These data might indeed show that particular cognitive assumptions of this victimological self-definition are empirically invalid. The sociologist can also present different interpretations that exist and that are possible in society as to the meaning of the distribution of income. Thus the professors think that they are underpaid because they attach great importance to what they are doing, while the trustees think that the professors are overpaid because, compared to business, academic activity is of little practical use, or because professors are deemed to be lazy bums or effete pinkos, or because holding down academic salaries is part of the war against inflation. There is no way by which the sociologist can make some final arbitration among these various interpretations of the situation; methodologically, he is limited to his own "second-order" interpretations. Thus there is no conceivable sociological or other scientific procedure at the end of which one may conclude that professors are or are not victims, are or are not underpaid—and thus no procedure by which either the professors or the trustees can be said to be in "false consciousness."

This, of course, is by no means to deny that one may ask who is finally "right" or "wrong," or even what finally is the "truth" of the matter. But these questions can only be answered on the basis of value positions, philosophical or ethical, which are outside the scope of sociological inquiry—such as a position of the cultural value of economically impractical occupations or the equity of income distribution in general. There is no way by which the sociologist, *qua* sociologist, can say that the activity of a classics professor has greater value than that of a shoe manufacturer, or that a particular income distribution does or does not violate the requirements of social justice. These are normative questions on which sociology must always plead strict incompetence. But even on the cognitive level (that is, with regard to questions of what is, as against what ought to be) it is important to reiterate that the sociologist does not interpret "reality" but rather interprets various interpretations of "reality" (or "reality definitions"). "False consciousness" as a concept implies "correct consciousness," which in turn implies a direct access to "reality" which the sociologist cannot supply.

Nothing said above precludes the, as it were, pedagogical uses of sociology. The sociologist, be it as a teacher or in some other communicating role, can assist people in understanding other points of view and in obtaining a more comprehensive view of the social world. This widening of people's perspective, let it be stipulated, is civilizing, even humanizing. Thus it is appropriate that sociology has a place in liberal arts curricula. But, as the sociologist presents a spectrum of meanings and values, he cannot tell people whether they should or should not adopt these meanings and values as their own. Or rather, the moment he does that, he ceases to be a scientist and becomes something else—advocate, prophet, even "educator." In these roles, he moves within a different relevance structure, and he deceives his public if he pretends that this different relevance structure is the same as the relevance structure of sociology.

Yet within the frame of reference of sociology, precise though its boundaries are, there are ways by which the relativity of the social world is transcended (though the transcendence is always *ad hoc* or *pro tem*). Sociology is not and cannot be a magical escape from the historicity of social forms in which meanings are embodied. The sociologist, like everyone else, cannot escape the relativities of his location in time and space. But part and parcel of the sociologist's enterprise is *comparison*. If the sociologist compares different societies and their different meaning systems, he *ipso facto* assumes that there is a plane on which such comparison is possible, and this assumption is part of his relevance structure while doing sociology. There is a further implication to this—namely, that *all* human societies and meaning systems have some things in common. This implication constitutes a transcendence of radical relativism, which, if adopted, would make it impossible to compare anything with anything.

Put differently, one cannot compare apples and oranges, except insofar as both are perceived as species of fruit. In the case of sociology, the plane on which comparison is possible is that of the universalities of the human life-world and its configurations of action— or, if one prefers, the plane of the human condition. As soon as one employs this phrase, one implies a certain transcendence of relativity—that is, one implies a human commonality that will reappear ever again despite the bewildering variety of social constructions. At this point sociology borders on philosophical anthropology and on the phenomenological analysis of the life-world. But it should be emphasized that this plane of the *condition humaine* is very abstract. It transcends time and space, and *therefore* does not express the historically concrete meaning systems in their relativity. It transcends this relativity, but it also allows them their place in concrete human experience.

There would be little point burdening this discussion with an attempt to delineate sharply the boundary of sociological theory and this kind of philosophical exploration. In practice, no doubt, the boundary is somewhat fluid. The important point to make is that sociology, while it borders on the great philosophical questions as to the human condition (the Kantian "what is man?"), cannot on its own negotiate these questions. It is and remains an empirical science, caught therefore in historical concreteness and its relativities. Sociology cannot solve the problem of relativity in the sense of arbitrating between conflicting meaning systems in terms of their ultimate truth. If such arbitration is possible at all, that task must be left to philosophy, ethics or theology.

These considerations bring us back to a point made before—that of the soberness and the modesty of the sociological enterprise. The usefulness of sociology for society at large (as against its usefulness to sociologists themselves) lies precisely in these qualities. Insofar as soberness and modesty may be considered moral qualities there is a certain affinity here between methodology and morality. There is another moral—or at least protomoral—aspect to sociology. It fosters attention and thus at least a potential respect for the immense variety of human meanings. The sociological act of listening requires at least a pretense of respect. It happens frequently that the pretense becomes real. That is, one begins to listen attentively simply because this is one of the requirements of research, but after one has listened for a while, one actually feels the respect that one has first evinced as a research mannerism. As the sociologist comes to be impressed by the variety of human meanings, he is also impressed by their precariousness. Just because all human worlds are "constructions," so they are fragile, contingent and finally destined to be swept away. The historian has long had a very similar sense of the grandeur and the tragedy of all human acts, but sociology adds a poignancy of its own to this recognition. In the end, every society can be seen as a precariously put together fabric of meanings by which human beings seek to find guidance for their lives, to be consoled and inspired, in the face of finitude and death. It is only one short step from this vision to the explicitly moral judgment that all human meanings of this kind have great value and should not be lightly discarded. One might even speak here of a specific form of humility that is the property of all authentic social scientists.

There is a paradox here: precisely when one insists that sociology as such cannot generate morality, the moral qualities potentially endemic in sociology come into view. Thus, albeit paradoxically, there is a bridge between method and vocation. Strictly speaking, the vocation of the sociologist is to do sociology. But as he does sociology, "cleanly" and without false pretensions, it turns out that this activity has human values over and beyond its strictly scientific purposes. These human values pertain to sociological research, but they also pertain to other exercises of the profession (notably teaching) and to the process of socialization involved in the professional training of young sociologists. *To be a listener of the many stories of human meanings—and then to retell the stories as faithfully as one is able—*this description of what a sociologist does is a restatement of certain methodological principles. It is *also* a statement with a certain moral status.

Again: sociology cannot offer moral guidance. Nevertheless, and paradoxically, it has a curious relation to ethics, or at least to a particular kind of ethics. This is what Max Weber called the *ethics of responsibility* (*Verantwortungsethik*)—that is, an ethics that derives its criteria for action from a calculus of probable consequences rather than from absolute principles. It is no accident that Weber *qua* moralist made such a strong plea for this type of ethics. To use another of his own concepts, there was a deep "elective affinity" (*Wahlverwandschaft*) between this moral choice and his understanding of sociological method. Why the affinity? Because sociology gives one a constant awareness of the force of consequences, including and especially the force of (probable) unintended consequences. The moral absolutist, by contrast, dismisses or at least deemphasizes consequences: *Fiat iustitia, pereat mundus.* For this same reason, with impressive regularity, moral absolutists produce consequences that are diametrically opposed to their own intentions. Thus, again and again, the pacifist produces war, the rebel tyranny, the puritan license. Sociology, however tentatively, understands and can predict this ironical relation between motives and consequences. The "spirit of sociology," therefore, is akin to an ethics of responsibility, to a moral calculus of *probable* gains and *probable* costs. In any case, whatever the deeper affinity between sociology and this type of ethics, the sociologist can be ancillary to the latter much more readily than he can put himself in the service of any absolutist cause. After all, the weighing of consequences in terms of rationality is at the core of any sociological analysis. Thus, minimally, the sociologist can clarify the context of moral choices.

Back for a moment to a previous example: suppose there is a conflict of values between traditional notions of family honor and more modern notions of marriage, sexual mores and the husband-wife relationship—as there is today in Spain, in other Mediterranean countries and elsewhere in the world. Suppose that the sociologist is talking with someone who favors the defense of these traditional notions, perhaps in an organized way, even by means of a political crusade. Can the sociologist, *qua* sociologist, take sides in this conflict? No, of course not. Sociology cannot legitimate traditional honor any more than it can preach modernity. But what the sociologist *can* do is to explain to this neotraditionalist what the old values of honor are up against in a society that is undergoing the changes that Spain has been undergoing in recent decades—industrialization, urbanization, democracy, the mass influx of foreign tourists and of foreign ideas, the increase of women in the labor force, the decline of the birth rate. Very probably, the sociologist will have to tell this *caballero* of the old school that the future of these traditional values does not appear to be very bright. But let it not be assumed that *therefore* the sociologist must recommend an adaptation to modernity. The sociologist's advice can never go beyond "if . . . then" statements of a probabilistic kind, and if the *caballero* replies "Thank you very much, *señor,* but it is the lost cause which bestows the greatest honor," then the sociologist can say nothing whatever—not *qua* sociologist, anyway, though as a person he may deeply agree or deeply disagree with his conversation partner. Conversely, if the same sociologist is conversing with a modernist Spaniard, who sees the recent changes in Spanish society as progress pure and simple, it will be the task of the sociologist to draw attention to other consequences, and especially to consequences unintended by the progress-happy modernist—the disintegration of meanings by which people have previously lived, frustrations and *anomie,* the politics of resentment, cultural standardization and mediocrity, sharper antagonisms between different classes. And, needless to add, pointing to these phenomena does not in itself make the sociologist into a neotraditionalist. Ultimately, none of this sociological advice will assist anyone in making a moral and existential choice for or against the traditional code of honor. But, whichever choice is finally made, the individual who makes it will at least have a clearer idea of what he is up against. And that is no small contribution.

Morality and religion have been the two areas in which the effect of modern relativity have been most shattering, for reasons that are not hard to grasp. If there are any areas in which human beings have craved certainty, it is these—the first containing the norms of living, the second the ultimate values that make life worthwhile. For individuals, it is possible, the relativization of religion may be the graver matter; it is probably easier for an individual to live without a firm morality than without ultimate meanings. For society as a whole, though, the relativization of morality is probably the more serious matter, for it undermines the very foundation on which any human collectivity must rest. This point can be made clearer by looking at the phenomenon of pluralism—a situation in which communities with different meaning systems manage to coexist in civic peace. Pluralism has an intimate relation with relativity, since the very plurality of meaning systems weakens the plausibility structure of each. In American society, one may confidently say, *religious* pluralism has been managed very successfully. The peculiar American phrase "religious preference" eloquently expresses this pluralism: "My religious preference is Presbyterian." Or, more recently: "I'm into Buddhism." It can be argued that much of the present trouble of American society comes from a new onset of *moral* pluralism. It can then be predicted that this type of pluralism will be much harder to manage: "My moral preference is for the use of arson as a political tactic." Or: "I'm into ax murders."

Fascinating though this topic is, it cannot be further pursued here. But it is necessary that a closer look be taken at the relation of sociology to these two manifestations of modern relativity. The problem of the relativity of morals can readily be stated in sociological terms: *Once one recognizes the "constructedness" of moralities, how can one make moral judgments?*

It should be clear by now that moral judgments cannot be made from within a scientific frame of reference, be it that of sociology or any other empirical science (psychology, say, or history, or biology). What must be stressed now is that the *same* situation can be dealt with both in a scientific and a moral frame of reference; put differently, the *same* situation comes into view differently as these two relevance structures are applied to it (they are not, of course, the only possible two). Within the one relevance structure, there may be this proposition: "Members of political movement X, for the following stated and unstated reasons, employ arson as a tactic." Within the other relevance structure, one may propose: "The use of arson as a political tactic is wrong"—or, of course: "The use of arson as a political tactic is morally justified." In each of the latter two cases, there is likely to be a rationale undergirding the proposition, but this rationale will necessarily be quite different from the rational steps that led to the sociological proposition.

An analogy may be useful here. Both in everyday life and on the level of theoretical conceptualization, one may apply the different relevance structures of practical utility and of esthetic judgment. For example, I may say: "This is a very good coffee machine." What I mean by this statement refers to the practical utility of the machine: It makes coffee quickly, it rarely breaks down, it is of convenient size, it can take various kinds of filters and so on. But I may also say: "This coffee machine is ugly." The two statements pertain to altogether different frames of reference, and what is relevant to make the one is strictly irrelevant to make the other. Thus I may logically say: "Everything you have told me about how good this coffee machine is may well be true; I *still* say that it is ugly!" Or: "Yes, it's pretty ugly, but I don't need beauty in a coffee machine; all I care about is that I get my morning coffee as efficiently as possible." On the level of theoretical conceptualization, these ordinary statements can be enormously elaborated. Thus one may imagine that somewhere there is a research center where battalions of devoted engineers are at work to produce ever more efficient coffee machines, and one may further imagine that these people have over the years developed a theory of coffee-machine engineering. But none of their efforts are likely to have much effect on someone whose interest is in the theory of esthetics (unless that individual adheres to the theory that functionality *is* beauty—a case of theoretical syncretism that may be noted but that does not contradict the discrepant relevance structures that divide all other estheticians from engineers).

Let us once more trot out our Spanish *caballero*: Don Jaime's wife has been sleeping with another man; Don Jaime believes that, to defend his honor, he has the right, perhaps even the obligation, to kill the lovers. (It is quite possible, of course, that, despite this belief, he refrains from doing anything about it—because he still loves his wife, because he is a coward, because he cannot handle pistols and so on. All these restraints are psychological or social factors in the situations, but none of them, to Don Jaime, negate the norm dictated by the code of honor, and are therefore irrelevant to the present considerations.) Now, let us quickly jump a few thousand miles to the west of that Iberian drama of passion—say, to Marin County, California: Jack's wife has been sleeping with another man; Jack registers for treatment in a "jealousy clinic." (Again, it is possible that Jack has had momentary impulses to commit homicide, but these are irrelevant to the norms that pertain to his actions. Indeed, insofar as they are relevant at all, this relevance has the opposite significance from Don Jaime's homicidal psychology: Jack would like to kill his wife, but this "hostility" is in itself a violation of the norm that points the way to therapy; Don Jaime shrinks from killing his wife, but this "unmanly" hesitation is a moral weakness to be overcome.)

An outsider coming into either situation is fully capable of interpreting it, provided the necessary research is undertaken. If the outsider is a sociologist, this interpretation, as has been shown, will take a distinctive form. Thus we can go back (perhaps with some fondness) to the Midwestern sociologist whom we left some time ago struggling with an invitation to an orgy. Leave aside the question whether she undergoes the greater culture shock in Spain or in California. More to the point, she can take very specific steps in order to provide a sociological interpretation of either situation. Let us now further assume that this individual has included the sociology of knowledge in her conceptual arsenal. After a while, then, she will emerge with, alternatively, a theory of sexual morality in Marin County and an analogous theory that pertains to Santiago de Compostella. Indeed, if properly funded, she may come up with a theory covering both cases, and that comparison may be useful in shedding light on the institutional factors determining sexual morality in general. For instance, she may come up with the following statistically buttressed proposition: there is an inverse relationship between the incidence of wife killings and the participation of wives in the labor force. In any case, let it be stipulated that our sociologist is successful in supplying a comprehensive and empirically valid interpretation of these situations.

The key point is that none of this interpretation can be directly used either to praise or to condemn either one of the two husbands. Put differently, both Don Jaime and Jack, being intelligent men, can read and understand this dissertation—without being swayed from their respective moral convictions. If the author of the dissertation continues to say, of either or both situations, "This is wrong," how can she do this? Very likely, she made this judgment before she even began her analysis. But, regardless of whether it is the same or a different moral judgment from the one she made in the beginning, her statement "This is wrong" belongs in a different relevance structure from the one that pertains to her proposition about women in the labor force. Take Don Jaime's case: our sociologist, presumably, believes that homicide is not a morally acceptable response to adultery. Or, in Jack's case: she believes that jealousy is a "natural" human emotion that does not call for therapy. Clearly, either belief presupposes a notion as to the "right" relationship between husbands and wives—let us call it a moderately monogamous ethic. But, in applying this ethic to situations far removed from Minnesota, our sociologist is implicitly or explicitly *positing* a universally valid human condition. On the basis of this, she then *decides* that the actions in question are not compatible with this view of the human condition. The more sociologically sophisticated our sociologist is, the more explicit will be (or should be) her positing and her decision. The grounds for the decision may vary. They may be religious or philosophical, or they may lie in a less elaborated conception of what is humanly acceptable. Obviously this is not the place to enumerate or analyze the different grounds for moral judgment. The point is simply that *none* of these grounds are either removed or fortified by the sociological analysis undertaken. Thus our sociologist, having successfully defended her dissertation, thinks once more of Don Jaime and, one more time, says to herself: "The bastard!" Or, thinking of Jack, says: "The poor slob!"

If we wanted to complicate the matter further, we could imagine that Don Jaime and Jack are also sociologists themselves—and they are making a study of the sexual mores of Minnesota! It might then be stipulated that they too will be able to come up with a comprehensive theory for which the Minnesotan sociologist is a case in point. *Her* moral judgments of *them,* in other words, can also be analyzed sociologically and social-psychologically. But, once again, such analysis will not by itself provide the ethical criteria for an ultimate arbitration of the empirically available moral contradictions. (A fuller phenomenological analysis of this matter would have to make a distinction between the "noetic" and "noematic" aspects of moral judgment, but this must remain outside our present scope.)

Morality, as externally established norms and as internalized constituents of individual consciousness, is empirically available, and therefore the proper subject matter of sociology as well as other empirical disciplines (including psychology). Ethics, on the other hand, is a normative discipline, which must have the purpose of arbitrating between empirically available moralities, be it on philosophical or possibly on theological grounds. Ethics and sociology, although they will of course often deal with the same phenomena, are therefore sharply discrete modes of intellectual analysis. This does *not* mean, however, that they have no mutual effect whatever. Sociology affects ethics precisely because it makes the ethicist aware of the empirical relativity of moral beliefs. While this awareness, as we have gone to some lengths to show, does not by itself lead to ethical propositions, it necessarily pushes the ethicist to look for criteria that will apply to all the competing moral systems that the sociologist can explore and explain. Put simply, sociology is useful to ethics because it makes the latter sensitive to its own location in space and time. One may also say that, in consequence, sociology pushes ethics toward a cross-cultural conception of universal norms. Furthermore, as was discussed before, sociology is particularly relevant to any "ethics of responsibility," because it increases awareness of the consequences, intended and unintended, of human actions. All of this, from the viewpoint of ethics, is by way of prolegomena. It is a significant contribution all the same.

Conversely, ethics has an effect, not so much on sociology as a discipline as on the individual sociologist in the exercise of his vocation. *Qua* sociologist, this individual is tied to the norms of the sociological profession, the "community of investigators." But the sociologist, as we have seen, has a "dual citizenship"—that is, he is also an ordinary member of society and as such is subject to the same ethical norms as anyone else. Ethics then must concern itself with the moral responsibility of the individual sociologist for his work and its uses or misuses—not now *vis-à-vis* the "community of investigators" only, but to the general public.

We can only deal very briefly with the other strategic question, that of the relation between sociology and religion. Here too, of course, the problem of relativity is central. It has been raised most sharply by historical scholarship in the area of religion, but sociology has added its own dimension to the problem. The problem can be stated as follows: *Can one still ask about religious truth once one has recognized that religious systems too are social constructions?* That religious systems are such constructions—or, at any rate, are *also* such constructions, within the frame of reference of any empirical analysis—can be shown quite conclusively by the sociology of religion (which, within the discipline, is really a subsection of the sociology of knowledge). Does this end, once and for all, any discussion of religious affirmations on the level of metasociological reality?

The problem is comparable to the problem of the morality in the way in which sociological insight into the relativity and "constructedness" of human meaning systems challenges claims of absoluteness. But the case of religion is different in that the object of religious belief, in the understanding of the believer, is extramundane—that is, has a reality over and beyond the realities of human life. By contrast, it is quite possible to make moral judgments without any such extramundane assumptions. Again, though, the two cases are similar, in that sociology can neither validate nor invalidate any religious proposition insofar as the latter refers to extramundane reality—that is, just as one cannot derive ethical conclusions from sociology, so one cannot use sociology in the service of theology (or, for that matter, of atheism). Religiously speaking, sociology must always remain agnostic. The sociology of religion too remains agnostic; whatever it has to say about religious phenomena is within the framework of what is empirically available—which, by definition, excludes the gods. When sociological reasoning is used to arrive at atheistic conclusions, as has been done repeatedly since Feuerbach, the limits of properly scientific procedure are transgressed.

For example: I am a Muslim. Every day I publicly affirm, "There is no god but Allah, and Muhammad is his prophet." Now, suppose that I am also a sociologist and that I undertake an exhaustive analysis of the origins, functions and development of this creed. In other words, I work at producing a sociology of Islam. This may include analysis of the socioeconomic conditions of Arabia in the seventh century, of the social psychology of Arabian prophecy, of class struggles in the cities of Mecca and Medina, of imperial interventions and trade interests, and so on. Let it be stipulated that I'm successful in this enterprise and that I do indeed produce valuable new insights, and even causal explanations, as to the early history of Islam. Let it be further stipulated that a non-Muslim sociologist, using the same procedures, will arrive at the same conclusions— which means, among other things, that I obviously bracketed my Muslim faith while I was doing this sociological work. Having done all this, can I still be a Muslim?

The answer, in terms of the understanding of sociological method presented here, is a definite yes. How is this possible? Let us leave aside for the moment the fact that Islam, unlike other religious traditions, has thus far been inimical to any modern scientific explorations of its history (in that respect, Islam resembles Christianity before the nineteenth-century revolution in the historical scholarship of religion); let us assume that I am a "liberal Muslim." I will then have a particular sort of "dual citizenship" (as has been the case with so many Christian scholars of the last 150 years or so): on the one hand I am a citizen of the "republic of scholars," in which capacity I not only undertake my sociological research but do so in collaboration with non-Muslims. On the other hand, however, I continue to be a citizen of the *'umma,* the community of Islam, and it is in this capacity that I affirm the Muslim creed, prostrate myself in prayer and engage in all the other actions of Muslim piety. Once again, within my consciousness there are two discrete relevance structures between which I'm capable of "migrating." And each relevance structure, dealing with the same phenomena, also *contains the other.* Thus sociology explains the Muslim creed. But the Muslim creed imposes its own order of relevancies on the findings of sociology. For instance, at the conclusion of my sociological explorations, I may erupt in praise of Allah, who used the social conditions of the seventh century for His revelatory purposes! It cannot be emphasized strongly enough that this is *not* some sort of schizophrenia—no more so than the coexistence of other discrete relevance structures within consciousness.

Thus sociology cannot say, ever, whether or why one should be or become a Muslim. To affirm the Muslim creed will be a matter of *decision,* based on whatever theoretical or experiential grounds. The religious experience that is at the core of the condition of being a Muslim is, strictly speaking, "immune" to sociological analysis. That, however, is not the whole story.

All religious experience takes place within a social

context, even that of a hermit (who carries around with him an *internalized* social context). This social context, of course, is by means "immune" to sociological interpretation—no more and no less than the social context (that is, the plausibility structure) of any other human meanings. Nor is it possible to isolate some pure essence of religious experience that will then appear as independent of its social context. Even if I hypothesize that Muhammad's original experience of revelation constituted a startling *novum* in religious history, a "leap in being" (to use Eric Voegelin's term) that cannot be understood as a development out of anything that preceded it—even then I must reckon with the fact that, in Muhammad's account, the revelation came to him *in the Arabic language.* The implications of this fact, precisely in terms of the social context of Muhammad's experience, are vast indeed.

As a conscientious sociologist of religion, who understands the character of interpretation in Weberian terms, I will not only explore the social context of early Islam, but I will attempt, as far as my sources allow, a phenomenological description of the religious experience. I'm propelled to do this because only by this means can I understand the meaning of Muhammad's and his disciples' actions. In this very limited sense, I will indeed be doing "theology" (just as Weber did "theology" in his analysis, for instance, of Calvinism). But I do this, precisely, in quotation marks. The Muslim theologian will speak of the angel who spoke to Muhammad; I can only report on the alleged "angel" who allegedly "spoke" to Muhammad. Substitute brackets for quotation marks, and then I can say in phenomenological parlance: my description of Muslim religious experience must rigorously bracket the ultimate ontological status of this experience. What is available to me is Muhammad's and others' accounts of religious experience, which I can only register as meaningful contents of their consciousness. And what, of course, is also available to me is the antecedent social context as well as the consequences, intended and unintended, of the religious experience. What is emphatically *not* available to me, *qua* empirical scientist, is the angel as a supernatural being, the Quran as a revelatory entity descended from heaven, or (needless to say) Allah as the divine being who is the ultimate cause of these events.

At the same time, however, nothing I can say about these matters can finally "explain them away." Even within my phenomenological description of the religious experience, I must take cognizance of its intrinsic ontological intentionality. That is, I can never say that this experience "really means something else"—that "something else" being, say, the class interests of Muhammad's followers, or their political ambitions—or, for that matter, the psychic needs of Muhammad himself. I must let the objects of my inquiry "speak for themselves." Put differently, I must allow the meaning *sui generis* of what I am exploring. Regardless of whether Muhammad's faith is shared by me or not, I must accept *his* intentionality and not impose *mine*. And, if anything is clear, it is that Muhammad did *not* intend his experience to be "really" about any sociologically relevant interests whatever (which, at most, were ancillary or even unintended as against the paramount *religious* meanings). I undertake an altogether different step if I myself assent to what the object of my inquiry (here, Muhammad) is saying. That is, if I now remove the brackets and affirm the ontological status of the angel, the Quran and so on, I am moving into a radically different frame of reference. Indeed, I now engage in an act of faith. (Incidentally, this point of view can also be further elaborated by distinguishing the "noetic" and "noematic" aspects of religious experience: the sociology of religion is basically concerned with specific aspects of religious "noesis," and the "noema" of religious experience can only appear in it within the "brackets" of phenomenological description.)

Again, sociology and theology are two distinct disciplines, with severely discrete relevance structures. Sociology has no choice but to bracket the ontological status of religious affirmations, all of which, insofar as they are properly religious, are beyond the range of empirical availability. Theology (Muslim, Christian or what-have-you) makes no sense whatever *unless* these brackets are removed. This, one should think, is a rather simple matter; it is a measure of the continuing influence of Feuerbachian reductionism that there are many Christian theologians who have not grasped it. But, as in the case of the relation between sociology and ethics, sociology and theology do have an effect on each other. Minimally, a sociologically sensitized theologian will have to reckon with the "constructedness" of religious systems—and, minimally, this will preclude certain forms of theological fundamentalism that are unable to acknowledge this. And, as with the ethicist, the theologian who understands sociology will be propelled to search for those universally valid criteria of religious truth that will transcend the relativities of time and space. The great difficulties of such a search cannot concern us here. As to the converse influence of theology on sociology, it is less direct; one can certainly do a lot of sociology without any theological sensitivity at all. But at least the sociologist of religion will have to develop something of a "theological ear"—otherwise the act of listening, so crucial to interpretation, will not be possible. One may add that the sociology of religion is not so much of a subdiscipline as many contemporary sociologists think. Virtually all the classical sociologists understood—not only Weber, but also Durkheim, Simmel, Pareto and others—that religion is a central social phenomenon, since for most of human history it has been religion that has provided the ultimate meanings and values of life. The acquisition of a "theological ear" is then something more than a marginal skill for the interpretative sociologist.

4

SOCIOLOGICAL INTERPRETATION AND THE PROBLEM OF FREEDOM

The perspective of sociology discloses man's "bound-edness" in a twofold way. First, from the moment of birth man is always in a social context that "binds" him —that is, he finds himself at the center point of circles of social control extending from those "significant others" with whom he is in face-to-face interaction to remote megastructures that affect him in abstract and barely comprehensible ways. This elementary fact makes possible a statement of deceptive simplicity: man is in society. This society is experienced by him as a hard reality—outside himself, imposing itself upon him regardless of his hopes or wishes, precisely as an objective reality. This is what Emile Durkheim had in mind when he insisted that social facts are "things" (*choses*). The "thing"-like quality (*choseité*) of soci-ety is what, first of all, makes for its "binding" effect. The English word *bonds* expresses very eloquently what is at issue here: one cannot have the solidarity of other human beings, the bonds that tie one together with them, without the bondage of social controls over one's life. Put differently, there is no bonding between human beings without the effect of boundedness.

There is a second, equally important, aspect to this. It is the subjective experience of society, which is the result of socialization in every individual consciousness. Socialization can be seen as an enormously powerful process whereby the "objective" structures of the society "out there" are internalized within consciousness. The "out there" becomes an "in here." The details of this cannot concern us here; the basic theoretical framework for understanding this process in sociological terms may still be found in the work of George Herbert Mead. As a result of socialization, every individual may be seen as a product of his society, allowing another deceptively simple statement: society is in man. Among other things, this statement brings into view the second way in which man is "bounded" by society: it is society that places within his very consciousness the mental structures by which he apprehends the world—and apprehends himself. (These propositions, let it be said in passing, are neutral with regard to the question as to whether there are mental structures antecedent to socialization—for instance, structures of language. If there are, they are elements that enter into the process of socialization—the "binding" effect of which could then still be described in the general terms used above.)

Inevitably, sociology as an empirical science deals with the causal effects of both of these dimensions of society, the external and the internal, upon human actions and events. Inevitably, then, sociology appears as a "deterministic" perspective. It explains this or that action or event in terms of the causal chains extending backward in time both in the social context and in the socialized consciousness. Indeed, this "deterministic" quality of sociology is what frequently arouses people's hostility against the discipline. An individual who has strong moral convictions, for example, resents being told that these are the result of his class position. (Let this individual's resentment not be dismissed too quickly! There is a good deal of justification for it—a point to which we will return.) Especially in societies, such as those of the modern West, in which great value is placed on individual autonomy and on institutions designed to protect it, sociology can easily be resented as a perspective set on showing up this value as an illusion; indeed, sociology could even be seen as an enemy of freedom.

A good example of this "antilibertarian" aspect of sociology can be found in the debates over the character of legal punishment. The fundamental legal systems of Western societies have been built on the foundation of a concept of individual responsibility (a concept both Judeo-Christian and Greco-Roman in origin). There can be little doubt but that the influence of sociological thinking on criminology, penology and jurisprudence itself has been to diminish the concept: if the actions and even the inner motives of an individual can be explained in terms of his social context and his socialization, in what sense can one still speak of his being *responsible* for a criminal act? As a result of this, legal punishment has increasingly come to be understood in pragmatic terms not tied to the concept of individual responsibility. It is important to see that both conservative and liberal theories of punishment fully concur on this, whatever other differences there may be between them. Thus both deterrence and rehabilitation are goals of punishment that require no concept of individual responsibility—both, if you will, could be applied to rats as readily as to human beings. It is quite understandable, then, that many have felt that this kind of sociological determinism undermines the moral foundation of Western societies.

It is perhaps clear by now that the understanding of sociological method presented here precludes this view of sociology, so that this kind of determinism (a positivistic kind) would be understood to be a *mis*application of sociological perspective. This, of course, does not change the empirical fact that sociology is indeed widely misapplied in this manner, so that one is left with a problem of vocation even if one feels that the problem of method has been satisfactorily solved.

But there is another strain in the sociological tradition that, both explicitly and implicitly, contradicts the aforesaid determinism. There is an undercurrent throughout the history of the discipline, an undercurrent precisely of resentment, even outrage, against society's oppression of individuals. It is quite likely that it is such resentment and outrage that has motivated many individuals to become sociologists in the first place, especially in America. This "libertarian" undercurrent, for the reasons just made clear, has always been in a certain tension with the theoretical formulations of sociology and has found it difficult to express itself theoretically. Its empirical basis lies in the simple but vastly important fact that individual human beings do indeed rebel against society. Max Scheler placed great emphasis on man's capacity to say no to society; Georg Simmel dwelt on the paradox that man is always both inside and outside society; George Herbert Mead analyzed the internal dialectic between what he called the "I," the core of subjectivity, and the "me," the socialized self; and, of course, the entire Marxist tradition of alienation theory presupposes a state of potential freedom *from which* specific societal structures have alienated man. It is possible for human beings to rebel against society; thus the network of social controls is not perfect. And it is possible for human beings to think genuinely new thoughts; thus socialization is never complete.

At this point sociological theory again borders on philosophical anthropology, an area into which we cannot venture here in any depth. It must suffice to point out that it is there, rather than within sociology itself, that the answers must be sought to the determinism/freedom paradox in the human condition. We would contend that recent human biology, especially as philosophically interpreted by Helmut Plessner and Arnold Gehlen, can be helpful in this enterprise. *Homo sapiens* occupies a very peculiar position in the animal kingdom, and this is the root condition of his ability to say no to the world. Plessner has called this man's "eccentricity," already to be found in the biological blueprint of the species—man is not "given," the way every other animal is, but must ongoingly "achieve himself." It is in this "imbalance" between being and action that man's biological constitution makes room for the possibility of freedom. Mead dealt with very much the same topic when he discussed the peculiar fact that man is both a subject and an object to himself. If there is merit to these views, then we would assume that this has been so ever since *homo sapiens* appeared in the evolutionary process. That is, the capacity for freedom is an inherent and universal human trait. But in Western civilization, reaching a certain philosophical and political climax in the Enlightenment, this specific human trait has been elevated to a central, sometimes *the* central, element of humanity. The history of sociology has been deeply implicated in this philosophical and political revolution.

A minimal philosophical concept of freedom would propose that the human will can, essentially or in certain acts, transcend the systems of determination in which man finds himself. In an older philosophical language, at least certain human acts are their own cause, therefore cannot be explained by antecedent causal chains. Another way of saying it is that, unlike all other beings in the empirical world (leaving aside the putative special qualifications of gods and angels), human beings are capable of doing and thinking genuinely *new* things. This capacity is necessarily linked to the capacity of saying no—be it to supernatural forces, to the forces of nature, to one's own body, and of course to all aspects of society. Man can only be free by saying no, by negating, the various systems of determination within which he finds himself or (using the language of existentialism) into which he has been thrown. Man's freedom only makes sense if it implies this transcendence of causalities.

Now, one exceedingly important point must be made here (philosophically, it is a point rooted in the insights of Immanuel Kant): *Man's freedom is not some sort of hole in the fabric of causality.* Put differently, *the same act that may be perceived as free may also and at the same time be perceived as causally bound.* Two different perceptions are involved then, the first being attentive to man's subjective self-understanding as free, the second being attentive to the various systems of determination. The two perceptions are not logically contradictory, but they are sharply discrete. Both on the level of ordinary everyday consciousness, and on the level of theoretical reflection, two discrete relevance structures are involved, both applicable to the *same* phenomena. Clearly, the relevance structure of any empirical science is limited to perceptions of causal determination. Therefore: *Freedom cannot be disclosed by the methods of any empirical science; sociology most emphatically included.* For this reason, it would be an impossible undertaking to devise a type of sociology that would include within itself the category of freedom even in its minimal philosophical sense. What *is* possible is to insist, as we have done in previous chapters, that the perspective of sociology and of any other empirical science is always *partial* and that other perspectives are possible—including the perspective of human beings as acting freely.

Throughout human history there have been acts which were perceived both by the actors and by observers as constituting a *novum*. After centuries of patiently endured slavery, for example, a leader appears who induces the slaves to rise up in rebellion. After centuries of a meek yes to slavery, suddenly is heard a fierce no. Let it be assumed that the slaves engaged in this rebellion do indeed experience it as a totally new expression of their freedom, even as the discovery of their freedom. How will this event appear within the perspective of the empirical sciences? If the sociologist, or any other social scientist, follows the method of interpretation outlined before, he will of course have to note the self-understanding of the rebellious slaves. He will, that is, have to deal with "freedom" as a category in their consciousness. But he can only do so in quotation marks, or within phenomenological brackets; he can, *qua* sociologist, make no philosophical statement that would concede ontological status to their belief that they are expressing their freedom. Indeed, as a sociologist he will be obliged to look for anterior causes of this belief, in the social context and in the socialization of these people. Thus, he may come upon this or that rupture in the erstwhile network of social controls —changes in economic conditions, conflicts within the slaveholding class, foreign invasions, the influence of foreign ideas and so on. In other words, he will have to look for causes underlying this new belief in freedom. *Mutatis mutandis,* this will be so with other empirical sciences. Thus the psychologist will look for causes in the childhood experiences of the leader of the rebellion, or the biologist may look into the effects on the organism of a new diet introduced just before the rebellion. Everywhere, then, there will be causal chains and causal determinants. It would be a fundamental methodological error to look for freedom in whatever gaps are left over in the web of causal explanations. Rather, the rebels' freedom, if it exists, must exist in the *same* reality that is *also* subject to the various causal explanations. If any scientist ever met the rebel leader face to face, he could certainly *not* tell him, "My science proves your freedom"; but *neither* can he say, "Your sense of freedom is an illusion."

Once again, then, what is at issue here is the relation of different relevance structures. Any proposition about human freedom entails a passage from science to another realm of discourse, be it via subjective experience, faith or reason. For sociology specifically there is no way of dealing with human reality except within the framework of systems of *social* determination (as against, say, systems of psychological or biological determination)—but the framework is indeed one of social *determination*. At the same time, the sociologist who is cognizant of the limitations of his method will be careful to state to others as well as to himself that this method cannot be used to deny ontological validity to the category of freedom.

There are two ways in which sociology, *as* sociology, *can* deal with freedom. The first, of course, is by interpreting men's *beliefs* in freedom, and by analyzing the social context and the social consequences of these beliefs. This approach has been quite fully discussed before and no further reiteration of it here should be necessary. The approach, broadly speaking, is that of the sociology of knowledge. But there would also be a second approach, this time concentrating on the external setting and the objective constraints on actions based upon the belief in freedom. In this approach, the notion of freedom can be translated into a concept that is empirically available—namely, the concept of *options*. Sociology is fully capable of analyzing the range of options, or choices, in a specific social situation. Thus, comparing masters and slaves, it is sociologically possible to show that the former have far more options open to them than the latter, and that *in this sense* the masters have more freedom than the slaves. In the same manner, assuming that the slave rebellion was successful, a sociologist may validly say that the rebels had increased their freedom. Further, different large-scale societies can be compared in terms of their ranges of options. Thus it makes sense to say that modernization brings about an expansion of options and that therefore modern societies are more free than traditional ones. What must be strongly emphasized is that both approaches are value-free in the sense previously discussed—that is, sociology has no way of judging that a greater range of options is "better" or "more human" than a narrower range. And it must also be emphasized that neither approach can deal with freedom as an ontological category of human nature or the human condition. That is, sociology cannot supply either an ethical or a philosophical doctrine of freedom.

In the Western tradition, first reason (with the Greeks) and then science (since the onset of the modern era) have been seen as instruments of human liberation. The basic idea in this has always been that understanding determinations opens up the realm of freedom. This was classically stated in the Stoic doctrine that the individual's freedom rests on his ability to distinguish between what he can and what he cannot do. In the case of the slave, it may well be that the only area of freedom revealed by this reflection is an inner, a subjective one—the body may be in bondage, but the mind can soar into freedom. But reason and science can also disclose systems of determination open to active intervention. Thus the slave may "scientifically" study the social conditions of his enslavement, and out of this study develop a strategy for rebellion with a reasonable chance of success. The motto of this type of intellectual enterprise has always been "Know thy oppressor!"; its most elaborate modern example is Marxism understood as a "science of liberation."

This understanding of the liberating potential of sociology has been present from the beginnings of the discipline. Auguste Comte viewed all of science in this manner, sociology above all, in its assigned role as the new queen of the sciences. There is a continuing theme of this type in the later development of French sociology, including the Durkheim school. It is no accident that, after the separation of church and state in France in 1905, Durkheim was asked to write a textbook of civic morality for use in the public schools from which religious instruction had just been banished—a sort of republican catechism—or, if you will, a catechism of liberty! In milder, less messianic forms this notion of sociology as a liberating discipline has been very much present in the development of American sociology, linked as it has been with social reforms intended to spread the benefits of American democracy. And, of course, this theme is very much present wherever sociology is under the influence of Marxism (more precisely, of Marxism as a revolutionary ideology—needless to say, the theme takes on a different quality when Marxism becomes an ideology of the *status quo* of socialist regimes; even there, though, in whatever shaky relation to the empirical realities, there continues to be at least lip service to the idea that Marxism is a doctrine of human liberation).

In contemporary sociology, the liberationist or "emancipatory" self-understanding of sociology takes different forms. It is always there whenever sociology is linked to the advocacy of socialist revolution, no matter whether this takes properly Marxist or more eclectic theoretical forms. Sociology has also come to be linked to more individualistic, less political programs of liberation, in which case it has often employed the ideas and concepts of existentialism. One may think here of various *rapprochements* between sociology and the counterculture. Cutting across programs of individual and collective liberation has been sociological feminism in various forms. The same overlap between private and political concerns can be seen in sociologists dedicated to racial emancipation, notably black sociologists in America. And sociology is employed as "liberating knowledge" in different parts of the Third World. It will be clear by now that our understanding of sociological method does not allow a direct linkage of the discipline with *any* doctrine of liberation, and to this extent we must be critical of certain methodological positions taken within the aforementioned movements. We must, of course, be especially critical of any methodological position that claims immunity to the relativities of history—no matter whether the alleged cognitive elite is identified with women (or women whose consciousness has been "raised"), blacks, members of a Third World underclass, those who have undergone a certain kind of psychotherapeutic experience, or members of the "correct" branch of communism. Science is universalistic or it is no science at all, and if any scientific method shares in that universalistic quality, then one can never maintain that only women can study women, only blacks can study blacks, or only members of this or that communist cadre can understand political reality. All the same, these various liberationist uses of sociology cannot simply be dismissed as being in error pure and simple. There are valid points in the intended linkage between sociology and liberation, points which must be critically clarified.

There is a curious paradox in the relation of science and the ideal of liberation. Historically, in its Western development, science has been viewed as an instrument of freedom. And it cannot be denied that science has liberated people from various forms of "boundedness," which in a scientific perspective came to be understood as having been due to "superstition." One does not have to disparage this liberating potential in order to be critical of some of the more exaggerated claims made on behalf of science. For instance, it is hard not to approve a development whereby cattle disease is ascribed to bacterial infection rather than to malevolent magic caused by a poor old woman deemed to be a witch. But, quite apart from liberating people from "superstition," science has been a force for greater freedom by the vast power over the environment and over the human body itself that it has engendered. Liberation from pain, hunger, cold, back-breaking toil and early death—wherever this has taken place in the modern world, it can almost invariably be traced back, directly or indirectly, to the power of science. The list of such liberations could be extended considerably. But, paradoxically, science itself has produced institutions, systems of thought and eventually social-political programs that bind people even more than the "superstitions" they replaced.

It cannot be our concern here to look further into the question (forcefully raised by ecologists of late) of how far modern civilization through its scientific-technological institutions has *reduced* options in a manner detrimental to freedom—as in its "bondage" to high-energy modes of production and life-style. Nor can we pursue the question to what extent the disappearance of witches has been linked to the disappearance of saints, and the question of whether this development represents a net gain or a net loss for humanity (after all, devotion, self-sacrifice and love itself have been deemed superstitions by some). But the paradox is very visible in our immediate area of concern here, that of the relation of social thought to freedom. At the very beginning of sociology as a discipline there is the thought of Auguste Comte, sprung from the St. Simonian movement, carrier of an ideal of freedom that was linked to a social-political program aptly described by J. L. Talmon as "totalitarian democracy" —all of human life being subjected to the (allegedly benevolent) dictatorship of an elite of scientists. The same antilibertarian thrust is intrinsic, to the present day, in any social-political ideal of scientifically reconstructing society, and for a very simple reason: if science is supreme, then the scientist has a privileged status as against ordinary people; the rational course, then, is to give scientists as a group (however organized) greater political power than ordinary people. In other words, those endowed with the higher scientific knowledge should also be endowed with greater power in society: *The cognitive elite becomes a political elite.* The development of Marxism from an ideology of revolution to an ideology of dictatorship is, of course, a prime example of this development, from Marx's "scientific socialism" to Lenin's "vanguard": if socialism is based on science, then the alleged scientists must be in control—the "vanguard" (in this case, identified with the Communist Party) is first of all a *cognitive* elite, then quite logically transformed into a political elite endowed with dictatorial power. Minimally, one can say, the social-political ideal of liberation through science has a built-in antidemocratic bias.

There is a general formula in all these developments —from a totalistic conception of science to totalitarian social engineering. Positivism and Marxism, despite their great differences, have this formula in common. In the case of positivism, freedom tends to disappear in rationality (may even be understood as an illusion); that is, if freedom means anything, it is to live in as rational a manner as possible and to rearrange society in accordance with rational principles. In the case of Marxism, freedom becomes an eschatological hope— the "leap into freedom" that will come with the revolution and the attainment of true communism—but *in the meantime* no freedom makes sense unless it is a step toward this ultimate culmination. The practical consequences of either position are remarkably similar, so that it is not surprising that positivistic and Marxist notions of rationality have been synthesized in an ingenious manner in the official ideology of the Soviet regime—the "Pavlovian" synthesis, if you will (never mind here that this synthesis does as much violence to the intentions of Marx as it does to the empirical canons of science).

There are vested interests in modern society, the vested interests of actual or aspiring "ruling classes," which makes such sociopolitical uses of science plausible. The problem of how to maintain the freedom of ordinary people against the dictatorial ambitions of these cognitive elites (from "scientific" social workers to "scientific" revolutionaries) is one of the foremost political problems of modern societies; indeed, the future of democracy depends on a solution to this problem. But the problem has its intellectual roots, as we have suggested, and the pretensions of all these putative elites can be criticized on the intellectual level.

This is why the view of scientific method (specifically, method in the sciences dealing with human reality) proposed here has very direct political implications. Just as a totalistic understanding of science adumbrates a totalitarian approach to political power, so *a nontotalistic, "modest" understanding of science is conducive to democracy.* Put differently, *by understanding science as a partial, "aspectual" approach to human reality, the scientist can never be accorded the status of a cognitive elite—and, in consequence, both the cognitive and the political rights of ordinary people are accorded the respect that is at the core of democracy.*

On the level of philosophical anthropology, there is a further constraint on such misuses of science—precisely in a nontotalistic understanding of man. If one perceives man as a being intrinsically "eccentric" (to use Helmut Plessner's term once again), standing simultaneously inside and outside society, and thus having the capacity to turn *against* society—then, on these grounds too, it becomes unthinkable to impose complete rational controls on human behavior by means of science. But this point cannot be pursued here.

On the contemporary scene, there are two major types of the "liberationist" emphasis in sociology—one individual, the other political. That is, sociology is understood as an instrument for the liberation of individuals, essentially in their private existence; or, sociology is to be a tool in this or that political struggle for a greater freedom of society as a whole. There are, of course, mixed cases, in which the quests for individual and collective liberation are deemed to be interlocked.

Taking the individual form first, it is very much part of a much more widespread phenomenon in Western cultures—the quest for personal self-realization. Very often couched in terminology and concepts derived from psychoanalysis (or, more precisely, the "left" or more optimistic wing of the psychoanalytic movement), there is a view of society as "repressive" of "healthy" existence. Liberation then means first seeing through the distortive ideas on which the repression is based, then throwing off the repression in actual living. In fidelity to the classical Freudian fixation on sexuality (though no longer bound by the Viennese pessimism of the orthodox Freudians), both repression and liberation are very often understood here as primarily referring to sexual expression, which is why this type of liberationism has been closely associated with the so-called sexual revolution in recent decades. Society, and especially Western society, has supposedly repressed healthy sexual expression by inculcating a variety of delusions in its members' minds. These delusions are to be debunked, and what follows this insight is a new praxis of sexual freedom. But the formula "repression-insight-liberation" is by no means limited to sexuality proper (as, indeed, it was not in Freudian orthodoxy either). Rather, it applies to all areas of individual existence—interpersonal relations of all sorts, child-rearing, attitudes to occupation and career, the pursuit of every variety of private "things" (from hobbies to religious experimentation).

Logically enough, the task assigned to sociology in this formula is the "insight" part. In other words, sociology, true to its debunking or unmasking tradition, is to pierce through the distortive ideas ("false consciousness," if you will) that previously legitimated the repressions in an individual's life, bringing about an experience of insight that is the prelude to liberation on the level of actual living (or, if you will, of "praxis"). Needless to say, there is a close connection here between theoretical insight and practical application—a "unity of theory and praxis," but in a quasi-Freudian rather than Marxist sense. More specifically, sociology allows the individual to perceive as artificial and therefore malleable those very structures of society that previously appeared to him in a taken-for-granted manner—inevitable, inflexible, "hard." Put differently, sociology reveals the "softness" of social structures, and thus allows the individuals to "step out" of those structures—first in the mind, then in action. Another way of calling this "stepping out" is "ecstasy"—*ekstasis*, "standing outside"/"stepping outside."

An important concept in all of this is that of *role*—a concept of central importance, of course, in American sociology and social psychology. Role here is, quite correctly, understood as the social patterning or programming of human activity. This concept is very logically linked to that of repression: it is an essential part of the repressive structure of society that individuals are so socialized that they automatically, unthinkingly follow the socially prescribed patterns or programs—they then "play their roles." Sociology analyzes these roles and discloses their "constructed" character. This insight has a practical implication: what has been constructed can be *re*constructed—or, for that matter, simply dismantled. This insight, when applied to a role that the individual may have been playing since early childhood, can have a blinding, shattering impact— "ecstatic" in the full, quasi-religious force of the word. And there can be no question about the fact that such "ecstatic" insight, and the liberated actions that may follow it, will be experienced by that individual as a great liberation. Theoretically put, the goal now becomes "role-free" existence—minimally, in one partic-

ular area of life only—maximally, in one's entire life.
In its maximal version, the goal is a salvific one—a
"leap into freedom" that transforms the individual's
relationship to self, others and world. In some
significant variants of this, even physical health is
deemed to be affected by this conversion experience.

Let us go back to an earlier example: many pages
back we left our young sociologist pondering her invitation to an orgy in a convention hotel. We have abandoned her in this uncomfortable condition, forcing her
to stay with us through endless deliberations of orgias-
tically irrelevant methodology. Let us finally liberate
our imagination, and liberate her, in an act of true ecstasy: *Let her, at last, accept the invitation!* She follows her colleague to the by now mythical fourteenth
floor, she enters the room where, behind the hotel-
green door of bland anonymity, the unspeakable out-
rages to bourgeois morality are being perpetrated. She
enters, she gasps, she joins in. At this point, since pruri-
ent interest is (perhaps regrettably) only marginal to
our relevance structure, we will refrain from giving a
detailed clinical description of just what our newly liberated Minnesotan did for the next hour or two. Suffice
it to say that every few minutes another old taboo was
broken, another path of freedom entered upon. We will
have to assume, of course, that, in the course of this ecstasy, she abandoned her stance as a detached observer. Sociology, along with her clothes and her Middle American morality, was ecstatically flung aside.
But there is one strategically important point that we
must make here: *Sociology prepared her for all this.*

How so? Well, precisely in the manner we outlined
just now. For many hours of listening to lectures, reading books and articles and writing term papers, our
young sociologist had been instructed that "sexual
mores" are specific roles, inculcated through specific

socialization processes in specific societies. How well she remembers one of the first things she was taught in her soc-intro course, "Thomas's dictum": "If people define a situation as real, it is real in its consequences." What has been defined one way can be redefined another way. Indeed, if we want to imagine that the other sociologist, the one who issued the invitation to the orgy, had to engage in some efforts of persuasion, we can certainly imagine that she used sociological language to argue that her colleague's hesitations were irrational. And that is why, quite simply, a sociologist (or, at least, someone who has taken a few sociology courses) is a better bet for an invitation to an orgy than an individual who has not undergone this particular initiation into relativity.

We posit, then, that sociology did indeed prepare our friend (surely, by now, we can call her that!) for her first orgy. Let it also be posited that the experience, as advertised, was indeed both ecstatic and liberating. As she now returns home from California, it is not difficult to imagine further that this experience was a breakthrough with continuing consequences at least in the area of sex. That is, minimally, our sociologist now embarks on a liberated (or at least *more* liberated) sexual life-style. But it is also possible to imagine that, having broken through her old roles in this area, she may now break through old roles in other areas as well. She dresses differently, she ceases to go to church, she changes her politics, she worries less about her career, she develops new artistic interests. And it may well be that these innovations are experienced as liberations too. Maximally, she may not only stop worrying about her career, she may give it up completely. Let us leave her once again—ex-puritan, ex-Protestant, ex-sociologist—perhaps happily cavorting in a rural commune, or alternatively taking her first steps toward a new career as a corporation executive (we will only insist here, without elaboration, upon the empirical possibility of existentially liberated corporation executives).

What all this amounts to is that there are good grounds for saying that sociology can indeed be liberating in the sense used here: *Sociology does provide insight into all forms of social determination and thus opens up new areas of choice.* Whether one praises or blames sociology for this will, of course, depend on one's point of view; in the example, the sexual libertarian will praise what the conventional moralist will blame. The point here, though, is that the claims made for sociology on behalf of individual liberation cannot simply be dismissed as an error in understanding. It is all the more important to see the *limits* of such liberation. (It is not necessary to repeat here once again the previous argument that sociology as such cannot recommend a practical course of action: sociology can disclose areas of choice; it cannot recommend one choice over another.)

There are, first of all, the limits of the individual's social situation: not all options are *socially available* and not all are *socially feasible*. Thus, with all the liberating insights available to a college-educated Western individual today, some may still not easily present themselves as possible options: I may ponder the option of defining myself as gay, but the option of becoming a shaman may not even have entered my mind. Further, options that are clearly present in consciousness may have very slim chances of empirical realization as projects in society: I may clearly understand myself as a potential world conqueror, but I'm having great difficulty getting my Napoleonic movement off the ground. These limits are grounded in some basic social realities. Even the most liberated consciousness remains a *socialized* consciousness, and this very fact imposes limits. And there is no direct translation from options in the mind to options in society; however liberated my mind may be, the "thinglike" quality of society, its *choseité,* does not thereby disappear; it continues to constrain me and even my most grandiose projects.

There is another built-in limit to individual liberations: *All acts of choice, if they are not to be fugitive (almost dreamlike) experiences, must become embodied in social forms.* These social forms will engender new systems of determination; indeed, they will produce *new roles.* Put differently, *the goal of a "role-free" existence is empirically unrealizable.* In this lies the irony, perhaps the tragedy, of all projects of existential radicalism. The reason for this is simple but basic: human social life is impossible without some measure of order, and that in turn means that human activity must be organized in mutually recognizable and predictable patterns—organized, precisely, in roles. This is nothing more or less than the process sociology calls *institutionalization.* It is common to all human societies, though it is arguable that under modern conditions (due particularly to modern vehicles of communication) the process is greatly accelerated.

For example: suppose that I *did* break through the limits of my own socialized consciousness and the constraints of my social milieu to become a shaman. Even within my own mind there will be a process of habituation. The first shamanic ecstasy is more shattering than the second, the third less than the second, and by the fifteenth time I may be able to say with a measure of calm: "I can do this again" (according to Alfred Schutz, a very crucial capacity). But the others, who are the witnesses and perhaps the devotees of my shamanic performances, *also* become habituated. The first performance, perhaps, erupted in the midst of a conventional cocktail party. Suddenly, there I was, frothing at the mouth, rolling on the ground, shrieking out the message of the god. No doubt everyone was startled, shocked, even terrified. The situation, in other words, was genuinely role-free, at least in the sense that neither I nor the others present had at hand the roles that would allow one to deal with this experience on its own terms (other roles, such as the role of "dealing with someone who has just gone crazy," were of course at hand and may have been promptly performed). But, assuming that I keep on doing my shaman bit and assuming that at least some small coterie of other individuals is prepared to be interested in my performance, a different situation will inevitably come about. Here I am, going into my fifteenth shamanic ecstasy. I'm frothing, rolling about and shrieking as vigorously as I did the first time. But the reaction of the others is no longer the same. They are not much startled anymore. They now know what to expect. In one formulation or another they will say: "Here he goes again." In other words, *I am now playing a shaman role*—and those who witness my performance are playing some sort of complementary role, be it as devotees, curious bystanders or students of the psychology of religion. Whatever else this situation now is, it is very far from being role-free!

This description of institutionalization and role formation can be generalized across the spectrum of individual innovations, liberating or otherwise in its initial thrust. Orgies develop an etiquette, unconventional dress becomes a uniform, atheism becomes dogma, revolutionary movements become rigidly conservative organizations and so on. And, of course, each of these transformations engenders new roles, new conformities, new systems of determination, from the "repression" of which someone will someday want to be "liberated"! The children of orgiastic parents liberate themselves by becoming exclusive monogamists, the younger siblings of hippies wear dresses and business suits, and a new generation of elite Soviet youth finds it mind-blowingly daring to go to church. Perhaps there is in all of this some of the fundamental pathos of the human condition. It was only the first time, when Adam and Eve saw each other, that the whole world was created afresh. There are dawn experiences that cannot be repeated. This is why childhood is such an awesome period—and why one cannot ever go back to it.

Be this as it may, if the foregoing is understood, then any totalistic concept of liberation becomes impossible. One will then recognize that any choice, however liberating when first made, will lead to new patterns that preclude other choices. Now, this by no means implies that *therefore* there are no genuine liberations. There are, as we have seen. But not only will one's expectations about the final import of these liberating choices be relatively modest and modestly relativistic; one will not expect total liberation. But also one will understand that there are no "free lunches." There are costs to be weighed, probable consequences to be assessed, *institutions* to be envisaged. And, perhaps most important, one individual's liberation may deepen another's limits. It is this last insight that, once again, makes one aware of the ethical ambiguity of all action in society —the awareness that underlies the previously discussed "ethics of responsibility." In terms of the present topic, *I am responsible for the consequences of my liberating choices.*

Once again: nothing said here necessarily challenges the empirical validity or the moral justification of any particular liberating project. But what is being said here must be critical of one recurring feature of much contemporary liberationism—namely, its peculiar time axis, in which only *the present* is emphasized, and in which there is an unwillingness to look into the future and a notion that the past can be somehow canceled. Sociology provides a corrective to this "now" mentality, by disclosing the web of causes and consequences that link the individual both to predecessors and to successors. Once again, the sociological perspective suggests modesty, soberness, a respect for other people and their values—and a nonabsolutistic, nondogmatic understanding of one's own ecstasies.

The political form of the liberationist understanding of sociology also follows the general formula "repression —insight—liberation," except that each term in the formula has a collective rather than an individual content. Sociology is viewed as an instrument to bring about a society that will allow greater freedom to its members. Again, this may be a relatively modest goal (sociology in the service of gradualistic or less than total reformism) or the goal may take on the eschatological qualities of a "leap into freedom" and into a new humanity (sociology in the service of a radical revolutionary vision). And again, the part assigned to sociology proper in this formula is, of course, the supply of the "insight" that is to be the prelude to the liberationist praxis.

As in the individual understanding of sociology as a theory of liberation, there are valid aspects to this political version of liberationist sociology. First of all, there is the empirical correlation between sociology and democracy. The rise of sociology historically was closely correlated with the struggle for political democracy. And in the contemporary world, democracy, or at least a measure of democracy, appears to be the empirical condition *sine qua non* of the development of sociology as a discipline. Sociology in authoritarian or totalitarian societies tends to become a caricature of itself, an intellectual *castrato*—or it tends to go underground. The reasons for this are to be sought in the intrinsically "subversive" thrust of sociological interpretation and this has already been discussed.

More basically, sociology provides a greater understanding of the manner in which social structures operate, including structures deemed to be oppressive. For those who want to change or get rid of such structures, then, the old motto of "know thy enemy" applies. Sociology becomes "intelligence" about "the enemy," whoever that may be. The relation of sociology to revolution is quite similar, then, to the relation of espionage to military strategy.

In illustrating this political function of sociology, we may fall back on the classical prerevolutionary situation: say there is a Third World country in which the mass of the peasantry is economically exploited and politically repressed by a ruling oligarchy. A revolutionary movement seeks to organize peasants and, with this underground army and various allies outside the peasantry, to overthrow the oligarchy. Sociology can illuminate the economic and political structures of the *status quo,* especially their not always visible interrelations. All this sociological material can serve as intelligence for the revolutionary movement. It discloses both the strengths and the weak spots of the ruling class, thus suggesting dangers to be avoided and opportunities to be taken advantage of. Thus it may identify disaffected elements within the oligarchy who might become allies of the revolution. Also, the sociological material can serve a propaganda function, the economic and political data disclosed being used to inform the peasantry about the forces that oppress them, thus to "raise the consciousness" of the peasants (what in Latin America has been called *concientización*), to increase their anger and thus to mobilize them for revolutionary action. Let it be observed here in passing that, for sociological material to play this political role, it is not essential that the individual sociologists who produced it be partisans of the revolutionary cause. On the contrary, material "captured," as it were, from neutral or even hostile sources may be even more useful, because the nonpartisan source increases the chances of its reliability. The same logic, by the way, applies to the intelligence gathered by spies. Good espionage produces intelligence equally useful to friend or foe—which is why double agents are possible and why it is useful to capture the enemy's secret files.

Within the limits of its "if . . . then" logic, sociology can also be useful to the revolutionary movement in suggesting processes and organizational forms likely to produce certain desired results. Thus there exists by now a body of knowledge, explicitly or implicitly sociological in character, about the probable unfolding of a revolutionary situation—in terms, say, of the uses of terror, propaganda, the organization of underground cells, the infiltration of legitimate institutions and so on. Needless to say, the same body of knowledge can be and has been used in the service of counterrevolutionary praxis—say, by the secret police and armed forces of the oligarchy. Also, when sociology outside the revolutionary movement is institutionalized in an even relatively autonomous way—as in universities, research institutes, various publishing outlets—it can provide an ongoing critical function useful to the revolutionary cause, in that it will unmask various aspects of the existing power structure. This sort of institutionalized criticism often survives in authoritarian societies that fall short of totalitarianism. For just this reason it is very common to find that the legitimate or semilegitimate institutions of sociology, like those just named, constitute important foci for revolutionary strategy—and, conversely, become targets of repression when the power structure feels constrained to become tougher on the opposition. For the same reason, the communities of sociologists and sociology students in such situations frequently provide recruits and supporters for the revolutionary movement—and, with good reason, are objects of suspicion and surveillance on the part of the organs of repression.

What has just been sketched in terms of a situation of revolutionary ferment pertains, in a lower key, to more placid situations. Sociology, because of its intrinsic critical propensity, serves to unmask the uglier sides and the weaknesses of any *status quo,* and is politically useful to those who want to change the *status quo* in two ways—by providing intelligence about the terrain on which they are operating and by providing material that can mobilize those who feel disadvantaged. And, here too, the following point can be made: this critical function of sociology is enhanced by "objectivity" and "value-freeness," because then its findings and interpretations cannot so readily be dismissed as special-interest pleading. It is one irony among many in this area that this point runs counter to what so many liberationist sociologists believe about the relation of science and political commitment. For instance, sociological material about racial discrimination is more useful politically when provided by whites rather than blacks, studies on corporate malfeasance are more credible when they come from right-of-center rather than left-of-center social scientists and so on.

Most generally, sociological interpretation is possible only, as we have tried to show, when *alternatives* to the *status quo* are perceived. This perception is intrinsically destabilizing, because it inevitably suggests that these alternatives are, at least in principle, possible. "Things are not what they appear to be"; therefore, "things could be other than they are." At least potentially, such a perspective has political consequences, and wherever the *status quo* is deemed to be oppressive, it is quite valid to see these consequences as conducive to "liberation." So far, so good. But this is not the entire story.

Again, it is very important to see the *limits* of this potential political use of sociology. Once more, as discussed before, it is a fallacy to take sociological interpretations as normative prescriptions. Thus, in the situation described before, the sociologist may be able to show how the economy of the *latifundias* requires that the peasant laborers be paid subsistence wages or less, how the economic interests of the *latifundistas* are expressed and served by the political power structure, how foreign corporate interests in the country interlock with the domestic power structure and so on. But none of these social-scientific findings lead directly to the normative injunction, *"Therefore,* the peasants should rise in revolution." The peasants themselves may well arrive at this conclusion, once they have been told and understand the sociologist's findings, and that conclusion may be morally justified and politically realistic. But it is *also* possible that the peasants do *not* reach this conclusion. They may decide that, although things are bad, they are better than what they were in the previous generation; or they may feel that things could be made worse by a revolution that may not succeed; or they might even conclude that the revolutionaries are not trustworthy and that a *successful* revolution would be the greater evil as compared to the lesser evil of the *status quo;* or again, the peasants may have religious interests and values that make revolutionary action implausible. A sociologist committed to the revolutionary cause can, of course, argue against any of these definitions of the situation—but *qua* sociologist he is no more qualified in this argument than any of the peasants, and his sociological findings and interpretations are only relevant indirectly, as "background briefings," to the practical outcome of the debate for or against revolution.

The sociologist retains his "dual citizenship" even in the heat of political battle. He confuses the two "passports" at his peril. The peril is greatest when he is a partisan. Just then, in the service of a partisan cause, the sociologist is most useful *politically* when he objectively analyzes the situation, clarifies options and assesses the probable consequences of alternative courses of action. This is inherently a sober, modest enterprise, very much antagonistic to the role of prophet, propagandist or agitator. Now, this *by no means* implies that the sociologist, as a person, cannot be involved in partisan political action—even, under certain circumstances, in revolutionary activity. But his usefulness *qua* sociologist will depend upon the exercise of his critical faculties, including their application to the cause or movement that he espouses. This is not an easy role, but certainly not an impossible one. Its burden is comparable to that of a doctor who diagnoses the condition of a patient whom he loves—or, for that matter, of one he detests. Shortly after World War I Joseph Schumpeter was invited to serve *qua* social scientist on the commission set up by the new Weimar government to nationalize segments of the German economy. Schumpeter was opposed to this nationalization. When asked why he agreed to serve, he replied that if an individual wants to commit suicide, it is useful to have a doctor in attendance. By the same token, if one is a doctor and one's best friend is setting out on a hazardous mountain-climbing expedition, one will be most useful by issuing carefully objective medical prognoses and *not* by writing inspirational literature about the values of mountain climbing. It is actually likely that others can perform the latter task much better.

Beyond that, there is an inherent anti-utopian tendency in sociological thought. Sociologists know, or should know, about the unintended consequences of social action, about the latent functions and the limits of institutions, about the weight of the past and the ambiguities of power. It is quite possible that the sociologist, as a person, is inspired by this or that utopian vision. But his methodological and vocational training should always introduce an element of caution, even of doubt, into his own utopian imaginings. Sociology is always an attempt to grasp social *reality*—the hardness of things that eludes our wishes. This in itself will serve as a brake on the wilder excesses of utopianism.

Sociology, as a science, should never consider itself the sole or even primary guide to political action. It follows that sociology, as such, should never become the exclusive carrier of a political program. This norm applies to any program, of whatever ideological coloration—of the right as much as the left, revolutionary or conservative, or dedicated to any national, racial, sexual or religious liberation. "Socialist sociology" is as much a *contradictio in adiecto* as "sociological Americanism," as are "black sociology," "feminist sociology," "Christian sociology" and so on. The sociologist who would make of the discipline that kind of exclusionary program will logically have to excommunicate from sociology (or from its "true" segment that he alone represents) all those who do not agree with the program or who do not have the ascriptive status of the "true" in-group. Once such a procedure begins in earnest, sociology ceases to be itself. It becomes a sect or a tribe. When this happens, not only are the methodological presuppositions of the discipline violated. Ironically, its *political* usefulness comes to an end. Caught in sectarian or tribal particularisms, it can no longer represent itself as *anything but* an ideological legitimation of these particularistic interests. This is why "socialist sociologists" can only talk to themselves, as do the adherents of "patriotic sociology" (if such can be found anywhere), "black sociology," "feminist sociology" and so on. It will probably not be long before everyone, inside or outside these exclusionary coteries, will lose all interest in this futile enterprise.

There are various parts of the world where this kind of sociology has become common. Those who should be most concerned with correcting this situation are those whose political causes have inspired these developments. Some further ramifications of this will concern us in the next chapter. For now, it should be clear that there is indeed a relation between sociology and freedom, but the relation is more ambiguous and less direct than many contemporary liberationists have liked to think.

5

SOCIOLOGY BETWEEN TECHNOCRACY AND IDEOLOGY

As seen in the preceding chapter, sociology is not only an enterprise within the "republic of scholars," but also has wider existential, societal and indeed political uses. Among these, the most common today are technocratic and ideological. The purpose of this chapter is to draw boundaries between our understanding of sociology and these two applications of the discipline. It should be emphasized at the outset that the intent here is not polemical but clarifying. Nor is it the intent to deny the validity of any and all technocratic or ideological applications of the discipline. Rather, our concern is with those views in which sociology becomes totally absorbed in its technocratic or ideological uses, in which in fact sociology as a whole *becomes* either technical knowledge or ideological doctrine, and we are greatly troubled by the consequences of these transformations both for social science and for the society in which it is practiced.

By technocratic use we mean that sociology comes to be understood and applied as a technical body of knowledge in the service of "social engineering." The latter phrase is employed deliberately. For it points to the important fact that this kind of sociology has a much wider social context. It is part and parcel of that "engineering mentality" which is a strategic component of modern consciousness as shaped by the technological revolutions of recent centuries, first in Europe and now all over the world. This mentality, of course, originated in and is perfectly appropriate within the area of technology proper. One cannot have engineers without this mentality, and, assuming that one does not wish to dismantle the technological infrastructure of the modern world, it makes no sense to bemoan this mentality. The problem arises when there is a carryover of this mentality from the area of technology proper to other areas of human life. The main features of this engineering mind-set can be described without too much difficulty: an atomistic or "componential" approach to reality—the world is perceived as consisting of units that can be taken apart and put together again. Means and ends can readily be separated. There is a strong tendency toward abstract and preferably quantitative thinking. There is an attitude of problem solving or "tinkering"; any problem encountered is viewed as, in principle, soluble if only the proper technical procedures are to be found. With this goes an attitude of inventiveness and a positive valuation of innovation. There is a low level of affect or emotional involvement—engineers are "cool" types. There is a high value placed on what may be called "maximalization"—more product for less expenditure. There is also the capacity to deal with many things going on at the same time—the capacity to deal with "multirelationality."

This list of features could be expanded and described in much greater detail. There is no need to do this here. Suffice it to point out again that modern technology would be hard to imagine without individuals whose consciousness is shaped in this way, at least while they are on the job in the technical occupations of a modern society. The problem is that these features are no longer restricted to these technical job areas, but have spilled over into many other areas. The spillover that interests us here is part of this general process of technological or engineering "imperialism."

When sociology is placed in the service of technocracy, it almost automatically comes to be translated into the categories of the latter's distinctive mentality. There is, first of all, the expectation that sociology can be applied to practical concerns in the same way that, say, a body of aeronautical knowledge can. This expectation puts a premium on the kind of sociology that can most easily be taken over in this manner—specifically, sociology of a strongly positivistic bent. Further, there will be pressure to produce immediately applicable "results." Such pressure is not just in some people's minds, but is socially reinforced by some sort of "fee for service" arrangement: the technocratic employer or client has a practical problem to be solved, and the sociologist is hired to find the solution. Not surprisingly, in terms of common social-psychological dynamics, this pressure tends to become internalized by sociologists who find themselves in this position. That is, the sociologists themselves now come to think of themselves as practical problem solvers or as "social engineers." Further, there now appears a commonly agreed-upon measure of the "success" of sociological inquiry, in terms of whether the products of this inquiry are applicable to whatever interests the "funding source." In this position, sociology not only becomes a tool of technocracy, but it is constrained to organize itself along technocratic lines. Roughly since World War II, first in America and then in other countries, sociologists have become accustomed to working in large, sometimes vast research organizations that closely resemble comparable organizations dealing with engineering concerns proper. Put graphically, as compared with the "hardware" engineers of modern technology, sociologists have become a subspecies of "software" engineers. While the two groups deal with different material and therefore have to use at least somewhat different methods, they come to resemble each other both in quality of mind and in the external character of their activity.

The technocratic use of sociology has frequently been criticized on moral grounds, because the goals or actions of the particular technocratic institution have been deemed to be morally objectionable. A well-known example of this was the debate over the so-called Project Camelot, when the American military covertly employed sociologists to engage in counterinsurgency research in Latin America. The ethical issues of this particular case need not concern us here. What is clear is this: if one posits, as we have, that the sociologist is responsible for the uses made of his findings, then there will be cases where moral criticisms are justified. But it is important to see that the technocratic use of sociology tends to introduce a deformation into the sociological enterprise *even if* the external purpose is beyond moral reproach. This is for methodological rather than ethical reasons: the integrity of the sociological way of seeing is subordinated here to purposes that are alien to it. At best, sociology in this position of technocratic subservience becomes a very parochial activity, situation-bound and pragmatic. The lessons of relativity and of the multiplicity of relevance structures in society tend to be lost, as the sociologist increasingly thinks like his technocratic employer or client. At worst, all the distinctive intellectual features of the discipline are sacrificed to the practical purpose at hand.

This does *not* mean that sociology cannot or should not be applied for wider societal, extrascientific purposes—even purposes of technocratic organizations, assuming that these are ethically defensible. But such application is always problematic, and the sociologist engaged in such activities should remain conscious of the fact. An analogy may be helpful here—the relation between artist and patron. A Renaissance prince, say, commissions a painter to do a portrait. Let us leave aside the ethical question that might arise because of the moral character of this particular prince; let us assume, in other words, that the prince is *not* Cesare Borgia, but rather a relatively acceptable character for whom the painter would not have to be ashamed to work. This assumption also implies that the commissioned portrait does not have, to the painter's knowledge, an intrinsically immoral purpose—such as depicting the prince as young and handsome, while he is in fact old and hunchbacked, in order to secure the hand of a princess to whom the portrait is to be sent. So far, so good. The artist decides to work for this patron with a good conscience. But there are built-in discrepancies between the two relevance structures of artist and patron. The artist, if he is a good artist, will be committed to a very specific vision of the world and very specific modes of conveying this vision by means of his brush. *His* relevance structure is this conception of his art, and nothing else. This cannot be the relevance structure of the patron, except perhaps in very rare cases. It is not only that the patron wants to "look good" in the portrait (though that will certainly create a problem for the conscientious painter). Much more broadly, there is the fact that the patron will have esthetic tastes that do not, cannot, correspond to those of the artist. The patron, say, wants a "pretty" picture; the artist wants to paint a "true" picture. Now, this is not to say that a reasonable compromise between the painter's artistic integrity and the patron's wishes could not be worked out. What is essential is that the artist be conscious of the built-in discrepancy of his situation. Unless he is so conscious, he will simply become the instrument of the patron's esthetic and perhaps paraesthetic purposes—and in the process lose his own integrity as an artist.

Back to sociology: the most vulgar deformation is when the sociologist, now more or less part of a technocratic organization, deliberately or (more likely) unconsciously adapts his findings to the wishes of that organization. A previously referred-to analogy may help in making this point: a good spy will provide intelligence that may or may not be what his employers want to hear. If his employers have any sense, they will insist that, in his reporting, the spy will pay no attention whatever to what he knows or thinks he knows about their wishes in the situation. This may work quite well in some espionage establishments. Knowledgeable critics of the Central Intelligence Agency have said that one of its major structural faults is that, within the same organization, information is gathered and various actions are taken on the basis of this information. In other words, "intelligence" and "operations" do not mix well in the same organization—for the simple reason that pressure is now generated to have the spy report what his "activist" employers want to hear. Similarly, the sociologist who has become adapted to a technocratic organization is pressured to produce less than reliable information and interpretations—and thus, paradoxically, he becomes less useful to his "patron." Generalizing from this example, it can be said that sociology will be most *useful,* even useful to various "patrons," if it is allowed to do its work on its own ground, that is, within its own relevance structure. To make this possible, the sociologist must avoid being sucked into the technocratic mentality. And, since mentality and social context are closely related (the root insight, after all, of the sociology of knowledge), it is probably advisable that the sociologist have his base in an institutional setting that is not itself technocratic.

There is another consequence to the technocratic use of sociology: pressure to produce sociology that looks as much as possible like the natural sciences that have proven to be so amenable to technocratic purposes. This means an affinity with positivistic sociology. This involves a cult of quantification—in the extreme case, a position that any sociological propositions that cannot be couched in mathematical terms are "soft," unscientific and useless. Note: as previously remarked, our position on the method of sociology in no way implies an antagonism to quantitative methods. There are certain sociological questions that are best explored by means of quantitative procedures, especially questions where the frequency distribution of this or that social phenomenon is relevant and where therefore statistical measures are relevant. The issue here is not quantification as such, but the *cult* of quantification, to the exclusion of other approaches. Further, there is the propensity to use obscure technical language, not because certain things cannot be said in common English, but because such linguistic esotericism is one of the characteristics of the natural sciences, which the sociologist must emulate in order to be taken seriously within the technocratic world. Finally, there is the mystique of the "expert," who stakes out a monopolistic territory in the social distribution of knowledge. As a result of this, there is the development of vested interests by bodies of experts—defending, expanding and selling their monopolistic (or, rather, hopefully monopolistic) claims. The details of this need not be pursued here.

Suffice it to say that sociology is part of what, since Fritz Machlup's work on this topic, has been called the "knowledge industry"—a rapidly expanding and very competitive sector of the economy of Western societies. Sociologists, by virtue of this economic location, are part of the "knowledge class" (also called New Class by some)—a culturally and politically important stratum in these same societies. Some of these developments may not be deemed objectionable, and it is not our purpose to polemicize against all of them in the name of a quasi-monastic ideal of "pure science." We only want to point out that these developments produce a degree of tension with regard to the previously discussed method and vocation of sociology.

But quite apart from the more vulgar deformations brought on by the technocratic use of sociology, there is something wrong with positivistic sociology *however used* (or not used at all). The basic fault of every form of positivism in the social sciences is the belief that the act of interpretation can be circumvented. This fault, of course, has no necessary connection with technocracy and its practical interests. It can equally well make its appearance in the form of a "pure science." The fault, as we have tried to show, lies in the failure to comprehend the peculiar character of human reality and, therefore, the peculiar character of any effort at describing and explaining this reality. Positivism seeks to grasp human reality in first-order rather than second-order concepts. One may concede that valid knowledge of certain kinds can be derived from such procedures. But in the end these procedures are unsatisfactory, because they cannot penetrate to what is specifically *human* in human reality—rather a serious fault in a science that takes this human reality as its avowed object! The resulting statements about society tend to be very abstract, far removed from the social reality of living human beings—and *therefore* neither very illuminating nor very useful. Again, the result is paradoxical: the very positivistic sociology fostered by technocracy tends to produce statements that the technocrats do not find very interesting, which in turn helps to discredit the sociological enterprise in the very organizations whose favor is being sought. This result, we believe, has much to do with the current malaise of the discipline and its lack of standing in the larger society.

This is the result if, so to speak, the public of sociology is *not* "conned." In a way, the result is worse if the public *is* conned. Then the sociologist may be accepted, not only as an expert in this or that area of "social engineering," but as a sort of general expert on the problems of living in society—a modernized realization of what Auguste Comte had in mind when he thought of sociologists as the priesthood of his new positivistic church. Then the deformations of positivism carry over into the everyday consciousness of ordinary people. Sociology, *qua* "sociologism," now becomes part—and an important part—of what may be called the "scientization" of everyday life, language and meanings.

In North America and Western Europe this broad vulgarization of sociology can be observed with ease. The educational system and the media of mass communication are the main purveyors of this practical wisdom. The deformation here is profound, because it now distorts not only scientific understanding but life itself. Put differently, "social engineering" becomes not just the (invariably part-time, professional) activity of a group of scientists but an existential praxis for large numbers of ordinary people. It is arguable that in this "scientization" of everyday life sociology still runs in second place after psychology (or, more accurately, "psychologism"). More people probably run their lives by the vulgarized categories of psychology than by those of sociology. This may be changing. In any case, the effects of the two vulgarizations are not overly different.

The individual in his everyday life now takes on the stance of an engineer with regard to others, including and especially those closest to him, and ultimately to himself. For example, children taught this kind of sociology in school and by the media begin to think of their own problems in terms of such categories as "identity quest," "intergenerational conflict" or "sexual life-style." In this, inevitably, there is a self-fulfilling prophecy. The individual who previously had not felt an "identity crisis" now develops one—often with deeply troubling results. Conflict between parents and children, posited as a normative reality, does in fact break out. Sexual experimentation, for which there actually may be no great desire, becomes *de rigueur* in a peer group thus indoctrinated. The reason all of this is a problem is not necessarily because the resultant patterns of thought and action are in themselves morally reprehensible or damaging. Rather, the more profound problem is that this attitude *in life* (as against such an attitude *in science*) distances the individual from social experience, from relations with others and finally from himself.

The scientization of everyday life implies a process of self-objectification and of alienation from the world, others and self. One now experiences oneself as a puppet in a network of social forces, a condition with which one tries to cope in an engineering attitude. Sexuality is a very clear case of this. One's own sexual desires and relations are approached in a mind-set appropriate to laboratory experiments. (This may or may not be immoral; what is certain is that it is anti-erotic!) Child rearing is another clear case. Observing certain parents deal with their children one can easily imagine that one is watching the unfolding of a technocratic design. But the same mentality is capable of extending into every area of interpersonal relations. "Role" and "life-style" become dominant categories now, but not as properly scientific categories of interpretation (as which, of course, they are very valid), but rather as existential guidelines. All of life, in the extreme case, may then be perceived as a laboratory in which the individual, in an attitude of cool detachment, tries on, puts over, tinkers with and abandons "roles" —and the human relationships within which these "roles" are performed. This extreme case, we may assume, is rarely reached. Real life is too powerful for this degree of self-alienation. But there are strong tendencies in this direction, and the consequences are troublesome without taking into account the extreme possibilities they adumbrate.

This process of the "scientization" of everyday life is itself institutionalized—via the educational system, the media, the law and (last, not least) the vast therapeutic apparatus. Thus children are taught that they are playing "adolescent roles"—and they oblige. Husbands and wives re-enact sociologistic models of "marital interaction" presented to them on television. Criminals disclaim responsibility for their actions by pointing to this or that social determination in their background—and the law, *mirabile dictu,* often accepts this position. And people who turn to social workers, guidance counselors and other "helping professions" with some of the perennial problems of human life find these problems translated into a jargon that bears little resemblance to what originally disturbed them, but which does have the advantage of suggesting some tinkering procedures within the alleged expertise of the "helping professionals." Some of this, no doubt, is funny—a peculiarly modern variation on the *comédie humaine*. But some of it has aspects that, without exaggeration, can be called dehumanizing in the effect.

To repeat: human life contains a rich, powerful reality, which resists absorption into the "engineering mentality." Sexuality, parenthood, marriage and all the joys, sorrows and terrors of human existence are such that they will, ever again, break through the fragile constructions by which "social engineers" try to constrain and rationalize them. But to the extent that these engineering efforts are successful, everyday consciousness itself now becomes technocratic consciousness. This "imperialism" of technocracy, both in the mind and in social praxis, is one of the serious contradictions of modernity. Inevitably, there are resistances against this. These resistances, which in their final intentions are not just antitechnocratic but countermodernizing, have been present since the onset of the modern era. They are very powerful realities in societies just now undergoing modernization (it is impossible to understand the Third World without taking cognizance of countermodernization). There are some reasons to think that countermodernizing resistances have of late grown more strong in the advanced industrial societies of the West. Be this as it may, it would be unfortunate if sociology came to be identified with all that this resistance is against. Quite apart from professional vested interests and the future fate of sociology in the wider society, there is an essential methodological corrective to all these deformations: *It is to be aware of the discrete relevance structure of sociology —and, consequently, to understand that what is proper in science is not proper in life.*

By the ideological use of sociology is meant any attempt to make sociology into a meaning-giving instrument for political purposes (the term "political" may be taken very broadly here, as pertaining to any collective project in the public sphere). Some of the problems arising from such use have already been discussed in chapter 4, in connection with sociology in the service of this or that "liberation," but some additional points of a broader character are appropriate at this juncture of our argument.

In principle, such ideological use of sociology could be either conservative or revolutionary, either dedicated to the preservation of the *status quo* or to more or less radical changes. Today, for a variety of historical reasons, sociology is rarely used as a political ideology in defense of the *status quo* (except in the socialist countries where a sort of "sociology" functions as a subdivision of the Marxist dogma legitimating the regime). In North America and Western Europe the period since the mid-1960s brought about this change. Obviously the change was not limited to the discipline of sociology, but was a broad shift to the left in the intellectual milieu (more so in Europe than in America). Within sociology, the opening move might have been C. Wright Mills' slashing critique of structural-functionalism as an ideology of the *status quo*. In retrospect, Mills' analysis was probably correct, despite the fact that the leading American sociologists of that school were anything but conservatives in their own political outlook. It is probably fair to say that, even if unintentionally, the structural-functionalist approach has an affinity with a basically conservative position on social change. The concept of "system maintenance" illustrates this effect. Now, as structural-functionalist theorists pointed out at the time, to say that social forces tend to maintain the existing system is not to say that this is what they *ought* to do. Thus, to use structural-functionalist theory as a conservative ideology entails an illicit translation from description to prescription. Fair enough. But precisely this translation, typically unconscious, was often made. In that case, the descriptive statement that this or that aspect of society was "functioning" was taken as a normative statement that *therefore* society was acceptable as is. Empirically, it is safe to say that in the 1950s (a period that saw a vast expansion of sociology in academia and beyond) most sociologists in North America and Western Europe were not engaged in working for any sort of radical social change, and while most of them were certainly not conservative in terms of the prevailing political spectrum but rather broad liberals, their approach to change was mostly mildly reformist, incremental or gradualist. Again, of course, they were representative in this of a much wider intellectual climate.

Today, generally speaking, the *political* use (as distinguished from merely *technical* applications) of sociology is "on the left." This, of course, does not necessarily imply an adherence to Marxism or even socialism. It does imply a sharply critical attitude toward the existing institutional arrangements of Western societies and an inclination toward radical social change. Particularly in the United States this generally *gauchiste* tendency is complicated, and ideologically modified, by feminist and racial forms of critical radicalism. In all of these cases, sociology is supposed to uncover radical inequities in society and to be placed in the service of political activity to redress the resultant grievances. The *gauchisme* common to most of these versions of radical sociology is centered in a pervasive antagonism to capitalism and its institutions, an antagonism not limited to those who would call themselves Marxists or socialists.

Very frequently this type of ideological sociology presents itself as a rebellion against the technocratic use discussed before in this chapter. From being in the service of existing technocracies (of the state, the corporate system, and various allied bureaucratic structures), sociology should now be turned around to combat these same technocracies. In criticizing the technocratic use of sociology, people with this orientation would generally agree with a good deal of our own criticisms of this, understanding themselves as the antitechnocrats *par excellence*. This self-understanding undoubtedly has a certain empirical validity. Even though, willy-nilly, most of these people derive their livelihood from the very technocratic structures they attack (including the technocratized university), this is no reason to impugn the self-understanding of their critical function or the sincerity of their efforts to "subvert" these structures. Indeed, one might argue that, on the whole, they have done a pretty good job. The widespread demoralization of technocrats (including the corporate ones) in Western countries can at least in part be traced to the successful efforts of intellectuals, including sociologists, to "delegitimate" the existing technocracies.

It is all the more important to perceive one very important similarity between the two tendencies—that is, between the technocratic and the ideological uses of sociology: *In both cases an external relevance structure is imposed on the sociological enterprise.* And in both cases this external relevance structure is *pragmatic*— that is, it is not the imposition of a different theoretical frame of reference on sociology (as happens, for example, when psychologists or philosophers "annex" sociology), but the mobilization of sociology for practical goals. It should not be surprising, then, that, *mutatis mutandis,* there are some similar consequences. Put differently, the sociologist ensconced in the bowels of some technocratic organization has more in common with his confrere rapping away in revolutionary enclaves than either of them would care to see.

In both cases the sociological "way of seeing" is subsumed under the pragmatic imperative of obtaining "usable results." In both cases these results (typically unconsciously) are adapted to the pragmatic purpose at hand; as has been observed before, this typically does *not* involve any deliberate deception, but simply a response to the social and therefore cognitive pressures of the situation. And in both cases the specificity of the sociological "spirit" is absorbed into or greatly modified by something else—by, respectively, the "engineering mentality" previously discussed and the "revolutionary mentality" of whatever denomination. These processes, in a curious way, have as their result a similar circumvention of the act of interpretation. Both, for their different reasons, have great difficulty sustaining the intellectual discipline required by the act of interpretation. Consequently, both are very vulnerable to distortions of the empirical reality of the social world. Both technocracy and ideology further bring about a curiously similar type of cognitive elitism—in the one case of the "expert," in the other of whatever group defines itself as the "vanguard" of the revolutionary transformation sought. Finally, to the extent that a portion of the public is conned, there takes place an ideologization of everyday consciousness that has strong structural similarities with the scientization discussed before. Slogans, theoretical clichés, ready-made bits and pieces of the ideological scheme, are superimposed upon everyday life in society. To get a vivid idea of this one only has to put oneself down in the midst of this or that radicalized student subculture and listen to how people talk about their private lives, their sexuality, their children, their occupational problems and so on. One especially interesting aspect of this ideologization of everyday consciousness is what may be called "institutionalized rage": since most of the ideologies at issue here posit profound and intolerable grievances against society, the individuals dedicated to them are socialized into a state of anger that becomes habitual, is continuously at hand, and can therefore be activated quite mechanically whenever a situation is defined as appropriate for its expression.

In view of all this it is also not surprising that in some places (again both in Europe and America) there has emerged an amicable relationship and sometimes even an alliance between old-line "hard" positivists and revolutionary ideologists in the discipline. There are tangible gains for both sides in such a coalescence. The positivists, in their interpretive poverty, derive exciting meaning from the ideologists; one might say that they obtain relief from the cognitive malaise of their abstraction. The ideologists in turn can fall back upon positivistic methods to legitimate their status as "scientists." The paradigm for this not-so-strange affinity is the old ideal of a "scientific socialism," but other versions of this may be found today as well. Needless to say, there may also be concrete practical motives for this kind of rapprochement, as in academic politics; even then, though, it would usually be misleading to think of deliberately political conspiracies; affinities of this kind normally come about in more spontaneous, unreflected ways. Wherever achieved, this alliance has considerable power, constituting as it does a marriage between utopian hope and what appears to be scientific rigor. The climactic figure in this drama is the sociologist who *mathematically "proves"* this or that Marxist (or feminist, or black nationalist, or whatever) proposition. Enough has been said before about the nature of positivistic "proofs" to suggest skepticism about the scientific status of such achievements.

The general problem both in the technocratic and ideological uses of sociology is the relation between theory and praxis. In our view, there certainly can be a relation, but it is not a direct, "one-to-one" relation. Rather, it is a "broken" relation. The sociologist who is committed to any pragmatic project, be it technical or political, must remain aware of this "brokenness" if he is not to be pulled into a pragmatic mentality that in the end threatens the survival of the scientific attitude. Again, he must remain conscious of his "dual citizenship." Undoubtedly this requires a particular effort from the sociologist who is committed to a revolutionary vision of social change—more so than in the case of a sociologist in the service of technocracy, where cool detachment is more easily maintained both socially and psychologically. But even for the passionate revolutionary it remains true that science as such is not made for the practitioner—and that, precisely because of this, it will be most practically useful if it retains its cognitive integrity. It is only paradoxical in terms of much recent debate that it is the revolutionary, more than anyone else, who, if he desires to use sociology, has a strong interest in maintaining its autonomous, objective and indeed value-free character. Put differently, the more committed an individual is to a political cause, the more he should eschew the ideologization of whatever social science he deems useful for this cause.

These considerations apply to every form of ideological sociology, "liberationist" or not, "left" or "right." If at some future date the political climate among Western intellectuals should change and someone would want to construct, say, a "free-enterprise sociology," the same considerations will apply to that project. But the paradigmatic and also empirically most important case for the ideologization of social science, of course, is Marxism, with its fusion of utopian vision and "science," and its so-called unity of theory and praxis. Some remarks, therefore, should be made about it specifically.

We are not concerned here *either* with the merits of this particular utopian vision *or* with the empirical validity of this or that Marxist proposition. Thus one could hold our view of sociology as a science and fervently believe in the justice and desirability of socialism, or in the correctness of any number of Marxist interpretations of the contemporary world—say, on the inevitably imperialistic character of modern capitalism, or the political dominance of corporations in America, or class struggle as the basic political reality of Western societies. What *is* incompatible with the views presented here is the concept of the relation of theory and praxis held by Marx himself and the great majority of his followers since then. This concept has an intrinsically ideological character that is inimical to science as we understand it. Now, this is *not* to deny that Marx and later Marxists have produced scientifically valid findings and interpretations. In other words, it is quite possible (and, we believe, necessary) to disentangle the scientific and ideological elements in Marxism. When one does that, a very considerable contribution is made manifest. One need only mention the linkage of social-scientific theory, history and philosophical anthropology (especially in Marx's early works); the treatment of the relation between economic forces, class and power—and, indeed, what one could call the *discovery* of class as a prime sociohistorical reality; the theory of class interests and of the super-substructure scheme, laying as it did the foundations for any sociology of knowledge (even those versions of it that later turned away from Marxism); the creation of a sociological approach to history (including such specific interpretations as Marx's classical essay on the Eighteenth of Brumaire). Much of this has become the common property of the sociological tradition as a whole, including the Weberian stream in it. This contribution can continue to be valuable for sociologists of different persuasions, especially if they differentiate between the cruder forms of Marxism (such as Leninist "historical materialism") and more sophisticated forms of neo-Marxism, some of which have pronounced affinities with the notions of sociological interpretation proposed here.

The specific interpretations of the modern world where we differ from any form of Marxism or neo-Marxism are beyond the scope of this book. What we must stress is the clear boundary between our understanding of sociological method and any currently influential form of Marxism. This boundary is not essentially substantive. *Any* substantive proposition of Marxism can, in principle, be dealt with in the framework here proposed. Thus, for example, Marxist propositions on the correlation between capitalism and imperialism are "researchable" by means of social-scientific methods that we would fully approve of; using such methods, specific Marxist hypotheses on this matter could be either supported or falsified. Rather, the boundary is methodological. Marxism, because of its deeply rooted connection between utopian and scientific relevances, carries an ideological animus that ongoingly interferes with the sociological "way of seeing." Frequently this animus blinds and distorts the Marxist sociologist to crucial elements of social reality. Take, for example, the bizarre quest of Marxist sociologists in Western countries for an empirically unavailable "proletariat": because there was an ideological requirement for this class to exist, the most ingenious ways were devised in order to "discover" (put brutally, to invent) it. Or, for another example, take the remarkable inability of Marxist sociology to shed any light on the social reality of existing socialist societies —a reality that, of course, is very hard to reconcile with the ideology. In the most serious cases (and by no means only in the case of the legitimating ideologists in the Soviet Union and other socialist societies that tolerate something called "sociology") this attitude leads to closed, dogmatic systems of thought, which are the direct antithesis of science.

In these instances "sociology" becomes a deduction from the *a priori* principles given in the ideology, an unfolding of a "truth" already known. One then "knows" from the beginning what one is going to find; not surprisingly, one then proceeds to find it. Again, these are extreme cases (though not on that account, rare ones). But even if this or that variant is not yet dogmatic in this sense, there is always a totalistic tendency. The reason for this is, quite simply, the Marxist ideal of a theory that will be an all-embracing system —an ideal that bears an odd resemblance to the totalistic ideal of positivism. Against this, it is exceedingly important to insist upon the inevitably limited, "aspectual," "perspectival" character of sociological interpretation—and indeed of all sciences. The totalistic or systemic aspiration of Marxism inhibits the interpretation of empirically available meanings, because these are always placed (however arbitrarily) within an *a priori* relevance structure derived from the theoretical system as a whole. Because of this *a priori* character, every single falsification is potentially threatening to the system as a whole. This is why Marxists (in this very much like adherents of other closed, dogmatic systems) suffer from what one might call a chronic cognitive anxiety. When particular meanings in society do not fit into the theoretical system, the category of "false consciousness" is available to take care of the discrepancy. Thus, for example, when concrete individuals who, according to the Marxist theory, "should" belong to the proletariat empirically define themselves as belonging to the middle class, then they can be assigned the status of being in "false consciousness." This theoretical strategy is already implicit in the Marxist concept of the superstructure, allowing certain meanings to be interpreted as epiphenomena. By such strategies the system as a whole and specific subtheories within it are made immune to falsification.

The boundary here is particularly sharp because Marxism is not only a theoretical body but, by its own self-definition, a body of practical norms and programs of political action. This makes the problem of coexistence between Marxist and non-Marxist social scientists particularly difficult. The parallel here is not the coexistence between other social-scientific schools (even that between, say, positivists and Weberians), but that between proponents of discrepant theologies or religious positions. We cannot deal with this problem here (it obviously differs in different countries). All that we must insist upon here is the aforementioned methodological boundary, which is essential to our understanding of the sociological enterprise. Also, having taken Marxism as the paradigm for the ideologization of sociology, we will leave it to the reader to apply the paradigm to other current forms of ideologized sociology. He will not find this a difficult task.

All ideologized versions of sociology, and indeed all ideological systems, are inherently seductive. On the cruder level, this is because they make the intellectual enterprise easier—and not necessarily in a pejorative sense only. One of the basic drives of the human intellect is the drive for meaningful order—and ideological systems provide just such an order. Having readily applicable schemas of interpretation at hand makes the task of trying to grasp the endlessly fluid, often chaotic-seeming reality of the human world less burdensome. But there is a deeper level of seductiveness. Ideological systems provide what Max Scheler called *redemptive knowledge* (*Heilswissen*)—that is, knowledge that not only provides intellectual understanding but also provides existential hope and moral guidance. This is particularly seductive in an age of secularization and relativity, where the traditional religious bodies of "redemptive knowledge" have become implausible to many (especially to intellectuals) and where morality is a very uncertain business. Max Weber has drawn attention to the universal human need for theodicies—that is, for explanations and "answers" to the problem of suffering and injustice in the world. And Ernest Becker has argued that the whole history of modern sociology can be understood, at least in part, as a search for theodicy—or, as he called it, an explanation of the "structure of evil." Yet sociology in the way we understand it can never perform this task. It must always stop on the threshold of any statements that could, conceivably, be of the nature of a theodicy. What is more, an empirically oriented sociology will ever again have to conclude that there are no easily perceived solutions to various problems of society. As Weber understood very lucidly, this is the tragic element in the sociological perspective.

Thus it is both sociologically and psychologically understandable that individuals (perhaps especially if they are young) should be drawn to theoretical systems that purport to offer comprehensive "answers."

To understand is not to concur. However burdensome or frustrating this may be, intellectual honesty constrains one to insist that sociology cannot supply theodicies, that, when it comes to the final questions about human individual and collective existence, sociology must remain agnostic. There are different ways by which individual sociologists can come to terms with this fact—be it by adherence to a faith and to values that derive from outside their science, or (as was Weber's case) by cultivating a kind of stoicism. In either case, one of the ambivalent fruits of the sociological perspective is obtaining yet another angle on the *sentimiento trágico de la vida*—a sentiment that has not only burdens but also consolations, one of the consolations being an aversion to fanaticism.

6

SOCIOLOGY IN THE CRISIS OF THE MODERN WORLD

If we take our minds back many millennia, back into the dawn of history, we may imagine the appearance of the very first intellectual. After centuries during which people did nothing but rhythmically bang away with stone implements and keep the fires from going out, there was *someone* who interrupted these wholesome activities just long enough to have an idea, which he or she then proceeded to announce to the other members of the tribe. We can make a pretty good guess as to what that idea was: "The tribe is in a state of crisis!" Things have been that way ever since. Intellectuals have a vested interest in proclaiming crises, because this attracts the public's interest and gives legitimacy to the intellectuals' occupation, which is *to have* ideas—an occupation that depends upon subsidization and the practical utility of which is often doubted by those called upon to provide the subsidization. This is only mentioned here because all proclamations of a state of crisis should be greeted with skepticism. Most people live their lives with little reference to the crises diagnosed by the intellectuals, being more concerned with the age-old crises of personal existence—lust, parenthood, disease, aging and the like—to have much time left over to worry about the alleged maladies of the larger society. Still, this was probably true even in such periods as the last days of the Roman Empire, when the barbarian hordes poured across the borders and one Roman institution after another disappeared into oblivion—and those intellectuals who announced a crisis then may be rehabilitated posthumously.

When we speak, therefore, of the crisis of the modern world, we do so, not in ringing prophetic tones, but tentatively and skeptically—if you will, hypothetically. However, it is our view that modernity has entered a critical stage in its history and that this crisis is deepening. It would be impossible here to give a full presentation of this thesis (we have done so elsewhere), and some rather sketchy observations will have to suffice.

Modernity is not some dark mystery. It is a conglomeration of technological, economic, social and cognitive elements, all of which are empirically available to the historian and the social scientist. One may, from one's particular value position, praise modernity as the embodiment of "progress" or bemoan it as the "decline" of civilization. The empirical sciences can have no part in this sort of evaluation. They can only explore modernity as one sociohistorical phenomenon among others, try to understand its salient features and causal roots and possibly (always in a hypothetical "if . . . then" mode) predict at least some of its future developments. In that case, the most persuasive manner of understanding modernity is in terms of the transformation of human life brought on by the technological innovations of the last few centuries. The core, the moving "engine" of modernity, is the ongoing technological revolution. But the effects of this have gone far beyond the area of technology proper, having cataclysmically changed virtually all institutions, the most global and the most private, and penetrated into the inner consciousness of individuals. All these effects, including those within consciousness, are empirically available and thus subject to scientific inquiry.

There can be no doubt that modernity has been experienced by many people as bestowing great benefits and enriching human life. It is this experience that has given credibility to the idea of progress in the first place. The benefits of modernity have first of all been material—in vastly enhanced standards of living, in the eradication of hunger and diseases, in lowered mortality and lengthened life expectancy. But there have been nonmaterial benefits as well, including the idea of individual freedom that has been so central since the Enlightenment. At the same time, modernity has also been experienced (sometimes by the same people) as exacting severe costs. Some of these are material too, resulting from the dislocations that especially occur in the early stages of modernization. Others' costs are nonmaterial but no less troublesome on that account—the breakdown of traditional solidarities, the imposition of new roles and institutional patterns, the loss in the plausibility of old values and beliefs. At their most severe these costs plunge the individual into a condition of *anomie*—that is, a condition of rootlessness, disorientation, of no longer feeling at home in the world.

These discontents of modernity have, from the beginning, called forth resistances of various descriptions. Sometimes these have been violent and political, sometimes no more than the efforts of people to keep certain areas of their lives away from the transforming force of modernity. Such resistances to modernity took place in Europe at its very beginning; they go on today all over the Third World, and there are comparable phenomena in Western advanced industrial societies too. Thus the recent upsurge of a ferocious Islamic neotraditionalism in several countries, while like all historical phenomena of some magnitude it cannot be traced to one single cause, is at the least *also* a manifestation of resistance to modernity. In Western countries such phenomena as the counterculture, the more radical wings of the ecology movement and certain aspects of the new religious Orientalism (again, phenomena of complex causation) make much more sense if one perceives the countermodern elements present in them. Much of social-science theory on the modernization process has seen it as unilinear, irreversible, presumably invincible. This view, in our opinion, has to be revised. Modernization is always in a reciprocal relation with countermodernization—and has been from the beginning. There are oscillations in this relation, and at times one "party" to the dispute dominates, at times the other. The older modernization theory is right to the extent that, to date at any rate, modernization has been the prevailing force, with countermodernizing resistances typically delaying or modifying rather than reversing the modernization process. The reason for this is, rather simply, that the technological "engine" of contemporary society could not be reversed without virtually unthinkable dislocations and, once established, this core of the modern system radiates its effects outward into every institution with enormous power. But, it should be pointed out, the history of modernization to date is by no means an infallible guide to its future course, especially in view of the fact that non-Western cultures are now vitally involved in the drama.

If modernity today can be characterized as being in crisis, one of the factors justifying this statement is that countermodernizing forces have been on the rise, both in the Third World and in the West (the situation in the advanced industrial societies of the socialist world, a grouping more or less contained within the borders of the Soviet empire, has its own, very distinctive dynamic, which cannot be analyzed here). The upsurge of anticolonialist nationalism and cultural self-assertion in the Third World since the end of World War II has given birth to countermodernizing impulses of considerable force. These only rarely envisage a total reversal of modernization (Burma in the early period of the military dictatorship is one interesting example), but they do seek to arrest the carryover effects of the technological core into other areas of life—such as family, religion and even the political institutions. Much that goes under the name of African socialism, for instance, expresses this intention, as do the Gandhian movement in India and various neo-Buddhist movements in the Far East. In the West, the growing influence of the countermodernizing phenomena mentioned above has also had effects going far beyond the subcultures most directly identified with them. The success of ecologists in bringing the nuclear energy program to a virtual standstill in a number of Western countries is perhaps the most dramatic case in point.

Now, what we have just been discussing are vast historical forces, in the interplay of which sociology plays a very small part. Yet the contemporary situation of the discipline must be seen against this background. As we have argued before, sociology is a peculiarly modern phenomenon itself, a child of the Enlightenment, and its peculiar form of rational consciousness is itself a significant aspect of the modernization process. Thus, in the current dispute between modernity and countermodernity, sociologists have typically been on the modernizing side. They have been representatives of "progress," rationality and a debunking attitude toward traditional values and institutions. Of late, as countermodernizing tendencies have spread among Western intellectuals, there have been some "traitors to their class"—sociologists who have enthusiastically espoused various countercultural causes and movements—but they constitute a not very large minority. It can be argued (we have done so elsewhere) that socialist ideology (even Marxist "scientific socialism") synthesizes within itself both modernizing and countermodernizing themes, and that this explains a lot of its appeal. Be this as it may, most sociologists who have recently espoused socialism or Marxism come down on the modernizing side of the ledger on most issues; they too, in their own fashion, are children of the Enlightenment, opting for "progress" and rational control, and typically look upon traditional values as "superstitions" to be overcome. Thus sociology as a whole continues to be not only a modern phenomenon but a modernizing force.

Insofar as sociology is the carrier of a specifically modern form of consciousness (we would refer here, for example, to our previous discussion of relativity), this is inevitable. A "countermodern sociology" would be a self-contradictory entity (this does not mean that certain people may not be fiercely dedicated to self-contradictory viewpoints—there are always such people—but it does mean that there are strong pressures against such a combination, pressures intrinsic to the cognitive structures in play). But everything said in this book so far prohibits the self-understanding of sociology as an *ideology* of "progress," as *endorsing the values* of modernity. Within the relevance structure of sociology, modernity appears in the same way as any other social phenomenon and it has no privileged status as against its traditional or neotraditional alternatives. This is, or should be, very clear. What is not so clear is how sociology can understand its own modernizing effects—and, on the ethical level, how sociologists should deal with the (sometimes unintended) modernizing consequences of their vocational activity. This is what we must look at in this last chapter. Put starkly: *The crisis of modernity has disintegrative effects. Sociology has contributed to this disintegration. What does this mean? What should sociologists do about this?*

The integration of society has always been a central concern of sociology. One may say that the root question of sociology is: how is social order possible? The question is most obviously central in the work of Emile Durkheim and the subsequent development of French sociology, but in less explicit terms all the other sociological theorists have been concerned with it. It is hard to imagine how anyone could do sociology, even of a very limited sort, without implicitly dealing with this question. Conversely, the dynamics of the disintegration of social order has always been an important area of sociological interest: how and why does a social order fall apart? A sociologist will have to posit that the problem of social integration is intrinsic to human life (which is why, for example, the French sociologists of the Durkheim school were constantly going back and forth in their analyses between primitive and modern societies). Conversely, social disintegration is a recurring phenomenon in history. One classical sociologist in particular, Vilfredo Pareto, believed that cycles of integration and disintegration had something of the quality of sociohistorical laws—a positivistic notion that Max Weber, for instance, would reject on methodological grounds, but with many of the substantive aspects of which he would have been fully in agreement. Thus the disintegration of the world of classical antiquity, the problem of "why Rome fell," greatly preoccupied Pareto, as it has many other historians and social scientists.

If one assumes that there has been no biological mutation in *homo sapiens* since the beginning of recorded history, then Pareto and others (going all the way back to Thucydides, who wrote his history of the Peloponnesian war to serve as a lesson for future generations) were right in believing that, human nature being what it is, past developments can illuminate the present and project the future. Thus contemporary commentators, on all levels of sophistication, are fond of comparing, say, America with ancient Rome, or modern Israel with Sparta, or Maoism with some earlier revolution in Chinese history, and so on. Up to a point, such exercises in sociohistorical comparison can be useful. They become distortive at the point where they overlook the specifically new elements in a situation—in this case, the specific *nova* of modernity. Human beings are still human beings, even in the modern era; but modernity has also introduced some important innovations that do not allow a simple, one-by-one identification of modern with premodern phenomena. Thus, for example, a comparison of modern and premodern imperial states must take cognizance of the enormous expansion of political controls and military possibilities brought about by modern technology. The Romans had no nuclear weapons, the Spartans did not have the rapidity of movement of modern armor and no Chinese emperor had modern media of communication available in his efforts to mobilize the masses.

The specifically modern problems of social order are rooted in institutional developments, but these have also become internalized in specifically modern structures of consciousness. As Max Weber correctly understood, a crucial characteristic of modernity is rationality. Modernization, on the levels both of institutions and of consciousness, is in large part a process of what he called "rationalization." While the core of this process is technology (in turn made possible by the physical sciences), there are two other enormously powerful forces of "rationalization"—the capitalist market economy and the centralized bureaucratic state. There are significant differences between the rationality of, respectively, the engineer, the entrepreneur and the bureaucrat, but all three embody (Weber would say, are "carriers" of) a modern rational consciousness that directly clashes with earlier, traditional structures of consciousness. Much of recent history is the drama of these clashes. Going back once more to our previous discussion of the "engineering mentality," the rationalization of consciousness takes place, for instance, when technical notions of "makability," instrumentalism and problem solving are carried over from the area of technology proper to other areas of human life—ranging from politics to sexuality. In the political realm, then, the problem of order will be perceived as one of "social engineering," of rational management. This has far-reaching consequences, most of them unintended and unanticipated.

It would be an error to say that this rationalization of society is *in itself* a disintegrative force (as many traditionalists or neotraditionalists are wont to say). The rationalization of institutions and consciousness is compatible with social integration—unless or until the rationalized systems run into "problems"—that is, when for whatever reasons the systems no longer work as they are supposed to. When this happens, individuals are constrained to attend to the question of what these systems "mean." At this point the previously discussed relativized and relativizing consciousness greatly hinders the quest for "meaningful answers." The effect, *then*, is disintegrative. What follows is a "hollowing out" of societal values. The old values, while still being paid lip service, have lost their plausibility as motives and legitimations of action. They are now "empty forms," and by the same token they lose their old "binding" power. This is precisely the process which some have called *decadence*—a perfectly acceptable category within sociology, as long as it is understood in a descriptive rather than an evaluative sense. In the extreme case, symbols for which people were ready in the past to sacrifice their lives now become targets of satire or of games. Thus the proposition that Britain had become "decadent" was graphically illustrated in the 1960s when the Union Jack, for which the servants of the Empire had fought and died all over the world, appeared on the bottoms of blue jeans in "swinging London." Comparable American instances are not hard to find. On this level, there is indeed a resemblance to events in the past—as when, for example, Alcibiades and his sophisticated friends desecrated the religious symbols of Athens during a wild party (very "swinging," one may imagine) on the eve of the military expedition to Sicily. Again, what is specifically modern is the relation between rationalizing and relativizing consciousness and this kind of "desecration" of symbols.

To make this relation clearer, a very useful theoretical tool is Arnold Gehlen's general theory of institutions and its application to the modern situation. Very briefly, Gehlen understands human institutions as substitutes for the reliable instincts that *homo sapiens* lacks as compared to other mammals. This means that institutions function to provide firm and reliable programs that individuals can follow at a low level of awareness—automatically, unthinkingly, "spontaneously." In this connection Gehlen developed his two strategic concepts of "background" and "foreground." Every human society consists of a background of firmly programmed activity and a foreground in which individuals can innovate. The purpose of institutions is to "fill in" the background (*Hintergrundserfuellung*); indeed, institutionalization is the process by which items that were previously in the foreground—that is, were fully attended to and deliberately performed—are transposed into this background of automatized programs. Take something as seemingly superficial as etiquette: two men meet and shake hands. In the history of Western manners, very probably this little transaction goes back to the days of knightly combat: two knights, perhaps armed to the teeth, met and clasped their mailed fists—thus, at least for that brief moment, disarming each other in a show of nonhomicidal intentions. Such a scene, in the days of the knights, was presumably one of foreground activity. Those who engaged in it, one may assume, were carefully attentive to what they were doing and could have fully explained the meaning of their action. Somewhere along the line, perhaps even before knights disappeared forever from the stage of history, this handclasp became an unreflected, unthinking and *ipso facto* meaningless gesture, a ritual performed automatically on certain predefined occasions—such as strangers being introduced to each other. In other words, the gesture became *institutionalized*. This location in the background, though, is not irreversible. Imagine that shaking hands, much later, comes to be endowed with quite new meanings: say it comes to be identified with those holding a particular political position. At this point, to shake or not to shake hands is again a matter of deliberation and intense meaning; it is no longer an act that one can perform spontaneously. The item has been "retrieved" from the background; or, as Gehlen would say, it has become *deinstitutionalized*.

One important aspect of this is that *every act of deliberate attention to institutionalized behavior is an in-*

cipient deinstitutionalization. The reason for this is simple: if an individual begins to reflect, deliberate and weigh options in this particular area of life, then it soon becomes impossible for this individual to act in the spontaneous, self-assured manner that every institutional program requires. Gehlen's concept of deinstitutionalization is well illustrated by the classical joke of the man who was asked by a friend whether he sleeps with his beard above or below the blanket—and found himself promptly afflicted with insomnia, as he had to keep awake in order to find out how to place his beard. In social as in sexual life, in other words, overattentiveness leads to impotence. Now, the concepts of institutionalization and deinstitutionalization are applied by Gehlen universalistically to very different societies. They are not limited to modern society. What is peculiar to modern society is a very high degree of reflectiveness, deliberation and choice—all features of rationalized consciousness. Helmut Schelsky, a student of Gehlen's, coined the phrase "permanent reflectiveness" (*Dauerreflektion*) for this modern characteristic. Precisely this aspect of modern consciousness is inimical to institutions, of whatever content. Put differently, *modern societies are marked by a high degree of deinstitutionalization*—or, by an unusually large foreground area in social life. This also means, though, that modern social order is peculiarly unstable, unreliable, vulnerable to disintegration. Another way of putting this, perhaps in Paretian terms, is to say that modern society is prone to a peculiarly rapid form of decadence.

The general process of deinstitutionalization can be described as follows: an institutional system works until, for whatever reasons (these may be societal or extrasocietal), problems appear. That is, things don't work any more as they used to. At this point, both the problem and the institutional system in which it appeared force themselves upon consciousness. A new awareness appears. Individuals now think about what before they did unthinkingly. Now, this is not necessarily disintegrative or destabilizing yet —only incipiently or potentially so. For society may have at hand, or develop anew, cognitive and normative formulas that give answers to the new questions. In that case, the problem is solved—not necessarily on the practical level, but on the level of meaning. In other words, the problem has been absorbed by the legitimating apparatus of the system. If, however, such formulas or answers are not at hand, and cannot be developed anew, then the new awareness *will* be disintegrating. Attentiveness will now be focused on the background (*Hintergrund*) in such a way that it begins to fall apart—or, more accurately, certain segments of it will begin to fall apart. The old formulas for the cognitive and normative definition of reality become progressively implausible, unreal, hollow; *ipso facto* they lose their integrative power. Insofar as they are still ritually employed, that very usage becomes a symptom of decadence.

The entire process, as described in the preceding paragraph, can certainly take place in a premodern society. Imagine, for example, a society of what an earlier generation of ethnologists might have called happy, healthy savages. This means a society based on primitive technology and subsistence economy, nonliterate, with its institutions relatively undifferentiated and built around the kinship structure, permeated with unifying religious symbols and endowed with a strong sense of collective solidarity. By its very nature, such a society produces relatively few *internal* stimuli for social change—socialization tends to be successful, there are few deviants, potential social conflicts are tightly controlled by the collective solidarity. The problem, then, is likely to be *external*—that is, it comes from outside the social system itself. It could, for instance, be a natural disaster—say, a plague of locusts. Imagine that the locusts stay a long time, or return frequently, and do lasting damage to the primitive agrarian economy of this society. In fact, the society is forced to turn from cultivation to fishing for its subsistence. The social system, however, has been linked to cultivation from times immemorial. For instance, the stratification of the society has been based on the ownership of agriculturally useful land, involving not only economic privilege but status and political power. All at once, this form of stratification attracts critical attention. As a result of the economic shift, it becomes progressively implausible, irrelevant. If those who previously held a high position, by the old hierarchy of strata, now strive to hold on to it despite the changed circumstances (which were first purely external, but which now are beginning to be reflected upon in the consciousness of individuals), then a process of disintegration may be set in motion. Now, it is possible that an answer may be at hand: perhaps there had been a previous instance of such a disaster, reflected in a myth in which the old landowning class takes the lead in saving the society by turning to successful fishery, thereby retaining their old rank in the social hierarchy. Or, alternatively, some ingenious and perhaps charismatic member of this class may *invent* such a myth and successfully put it over on the rest of the tribe. It is also possible that such answers are not produced, or if produced, fail to convince. In that case the society may be on the brink of a social revolution. One important step leading to this revolution may well be the desecration of the symbols of the old order—with revolutionary intent by those wanting to take over the society (say, the new fishing class)—or, more interestingly, in a spirit of self-mocking demoralization by decadent members of the old elite.

Now, we have carefully omitted any element of modernity from this example. Suppose now that a comparable process takes place under the conditions of modernization. The same society just described is affected, again from the outside, by a modernizing change: these people turn to fishing, not because locusts have destroyed their previous agricultural economy, but because fish have suddenly become a valuable market commodity (assume that modernization has arrived in a capitalist version), or because (assuming a socialist or more *dirigiste* version of modernization) the government has decided that these people should turn to fishery. The problem that now appears, in terms of the traditional social system, is similar in many ways to the one described for the premodern example. What is different is that the new awareness, the new attentiveness to society (one could almost say, an incipient *sociological* perspective), is marked by a new kind of critical rationality. *Both* the entrepreneurship forced on the tribe by the intrusion of market economics *and* the bureaucratic patterns imposed by government intervention are rationalizing in a Weberian sense. If, as one can easily imagine, the economic shift is accompanied by the introduction of modern techniques of fishery, yet another rationalizing element will be introduced. It is not just the economy that becomes rationalized now. Very probably there will be a carryover into other institutions—and, most important, into consciousness itself. The new rational structures of consciousness are intrinsically inimical to the old answers—in this case, they are anti-mythological. Indeed, the new rationality will tend to debunk traditional beliefs and values in a direct and brutal manner. One can easily imagine the desecrations that will now be carried on, especially by younger individuals. What is more, whatever problems now appear in the social system, whatever their nature, will be approached in the new problem-solving attitude. In other words, the new answers will be highly rational themselves. Here, however, comes the rub. As we have seen before throughout the discussion of the distinctive form of rational consciousness called sociology, there are certain questions of the meaning of human life that rationality can only cope with very inadequately. Put simply, the new rationality cannot produce satisfactory values—except for the purely instrumental values, such as efficiency, maximalization and so on. Thus there appears a coexistence of instrumentalism and *anomie,* engineering pragmatism and decadence. In sum, our little tribe too has been initiated into the crisis of modernity!

It should not be difficult to see now in what sense sociology itself might be seen as a contributor to decadence and social disintegration—the diagnosis that is itself part of the disease.

Sociology is precisely one of the structures of modern consciousness that provide answers to the problems of social life—answers of the peculiarly modern type, with the characteristics and the limitations of this type of rationality. Sociology provides concepts and explanatory schemas by which the processes of change can be analyzed and explained. But, while it is doing this, it also *contributes* to the processes of change. It does so especially, of course, as soon as the peculiar sociological perspective is diffused (by teaching, writings, electronic media and what-have-you) beyond the scientific "community of investigators" to a broader public. In terms of the act of interpretation as we have previously described it, one may say, with a little poetic license, that in this diffusion the scientific "virtues" are prone to become cultural "vices."

The basic transformation that occurs here has already been described in our discussion of the "scientization" and "ideologization" of everyday life. It is the scientization variant of diffusion that is, in some way, the more interesting, because it apparently does not deviate from the canons of science, notably of scientific objectivity, while the ideologizers typically reject these canons. The diffusion of sociological findings and interpretations remains relatively harmless until it touches upon values and norms. When it touches on these, a specific change takes place: *Values become value data.* Put differently, *scientific value-freeness* (*perfectly proper within the scientific relevance structure*) *becomes value-freeness in everyday life* (*where it has no proper place*). In consequence, normative propositions are translated into cognitive ones. For example, the proposition "Old people should be treated with special respect" is translated into "In this tribe there has existed the norm that old people should be treated with special respect." The first proposition is a reiteration of the tribal morality; the second proposition simply describes what this morality has been, with no normative imperative being implied; what the second proposition implies instead is that the tribal morality could, after all, be different—and thus, however subtly and embryonically, it begins to deprive that morality of its normative status. Added to this, of course, is the intrinsically debunking and relativizing thrust of the sociological perspective. In consequence, an individual who internalizes these features, *without* the methodological bracketing that characterizes their scientific use, acquires an alienating distance to social reality. Values and beliefs are included in this distancing. Incipiently, at least, their plausibility comes to be undermined.

It cannot be strongly enough emphasized that it is the *same* features of sociology, which are appropriate to the scientific relevance structure, which now become highly problematic when transferred to the relevance structure of everyday life. Staying with the medical metaphor for a moment longer, it is like the migration of bacteria from one population, where they caused mild discomforts, to another population, where they brought on a virulent epidemic. Objective detachment, value-freeness, bracketing, cause/effect explanations, "if . . . then" logic applied to moral norms—all of these take on a very different character as they are translated from social science to everyday social life. From cognitive tools they are transformed into factors conducive to normative disintegration.

It is not necessary to reiterate here our previous description of the ensuing scientization of everyday life. Ideologization produces similar consequences. What must be stressed is that we have no wish to suggest that, because of all this, sociology should become a sort of secret science, restricted to a carefully screened circle of initiates, or that the public should be protected from the subversive possibilities inherent in the discipline by means of this or that procedure of censorship. Such notions are repugnant both to the openness of scientific inquiry and to elementary norms of democracy. What we *are* suggesting, though, is that it is part of the vocational responsibility of sociologists to take precautions against these abuses of their findings and interpretations. Methodological clarity is one of the preconditions of this responsibility.

"Pop sociology," in any of its variants, is dangerous. The basic error, to which we have felt constrained to return repeatedly, is the failure to see the hard boundaries between science and life. In the popularization of sociology, the discipline changes from being a method of analyzing the legitimating processes in society to itself being a legitimating or (more commonly today) *de*legitimating force. Because of its inherent limitations, sociology cannot plausibly legitimate anything. What it *can* do, with great popular effect, is to *de*legitimate. Thus sociology contributes to the disillusion, *anomie* and normative disintegration of modern society. This is a weighty matter and sociologists cannot shrug off their ensuing responsibility.

Also, sociology in this role contributes to the divisions in society—specifically, the division between those who continue to live by the old values (applying rationality to life in only a restricted way) and those who want to provide new values allegedly based on scientific rationality. As we have indicated before, the latter group in large measure coincides with a *specific class*—the "knowledge class" or "New Class"—that stratum in modern society deriving its livelihood from the production and distribution of symbolic knowledge rather than of material goods. As this class is engaged in various struggles with other classes, sociology becomes caught up in this class conflict. This in itself is an aberration for a vocation that defines itself as engaged in a scientific enterprise. But, even apart from this, the practical consequences of this involvement are likely to be unfortunate for the discipline. Already in the short run sociology is likely to lose its reputation as an objective form of inquiry as it can be shown up to be in the service of specific vested interests. In the long run, of course, the consequences will depend on the outcome of the class conflict. If the knowledge class succeeds in establishing itself as one of the elite strata in the society, then sociology would become an ideology of the new *status quo,* justifying the exercise of power by this new elite of rationalizers. That would be a sad fate for a discipline that has always prided itself for its critical attitude. Alternatively, there could be a violent "nativistic" reaction against the new knowledge class, in the form of a populist revolt (which could take either "right-wing" or "left-wing" forms) against intellectuals and their institutions. That too would be a deplorable prospect. Neither outcome is something to be looked forward to by anyone who values both science and democracy.

It is important to see that these broad effects of sociology are not just a matter of some individuals exercising an influence through their teaching or writing, though that too of course happens. It is sociology as an institutionalized form of consciousness that has these effects. That is, it is not sociologists as individuals but sociology as a profession that is at issue—over and beyond the obvious ethical proposition that individuals, also individual sociologists, are responsible for their actions. Sociology as a profession has a specific location in academia, in other intellectual settings (such as research institutes, therapeutic agencies and planning boards), in government, in the realm of political discourse and in the media of mass communication. Like any other profession, sociology has a vested interest in the plausibility and public prestige of the "answers" it is capable of supplying. Consequently, sociology has an interest in clarifying its public role, not only ethically but in terms of its institutional future. Needless to say, the sociologist who is concerned with the future of society as a whole will have an even stronger interest in such clarification.

A distinction must be made, ethically, between two situations in which sociologists may find themselves. The first is a situation in which values are more or less intact, the second one in which strong disintegration is evident. Obviously, there will be mixed cases, and then some sort of prudential judgment will have to be made as to which ethical considerations apply. For our purpose here it should suffice to look at the two situations as they occur in relatively pure form.

Suppose that I am a teacher of sociology in a small, denominational college in one of the less sophisticated regions of the country. The great majority of my students come from small towns or rural areas. The same majority is ethically and religiously homogeneous, and comes from a middle-class to lower-middle-class background. Assuming that the norms of academic freedom have been established in this college and I can teach what I want to teach, it is safe to assume that my sociology courses will be mildly disturbing to some of my students. It is even possible that for a few students, probably the more intelligent ones, the disturbance might be more serious; these students present a special ethical problem, comparable to the problem of the second situation. But most of my students in this milieu are unlikely to be severely shaken by what I have to tell them. Many of them will actually fail to make any existentially relevant translations from what is said in the classroom to what is done in "real life." By analogy, students in an introductory philosophy course may be intrigued when challenged by their teacher to prove the existence of a chair that nobody is looking at, but all the time they *know* that the chair is really there; in other words, they are just engaging in an intellectual game in the classroom. The same attitude can pertain to the game of sociology, restricted to the classroom and thus segregated from "real" concerns. Of course, some of the students will recognize that sociological notions of the "constructedness" and relativity of social worlds can be applied to their own world, and this will trouble them. But this world, in our example, is still a very strong world. Its cognitive definitions of reality and its moral norms continue to exercise a taken-for-granted dominance in the consciousness of these students, and it would take more than a few sociology courses to shake them loose from it. What is more, their social world has at hand explanations and legitimations still quite capable of taking care of whatever cognitive dissonance I'm producing. My teaching, then, may have little or no existential consequences for these students. Or, even better from a pedagogical viewpoint, I may succeed in broadening them a little, freeing them from a few of the more obscurantist elements of their happy provincialism, without plunging them into an existential crisis. Therefore, I need not torture myself with ethical qualms about the disintegrative effects of my sociology.

But suppose now that I am a teacher of sociology in a large state university, or in an elite or metropolitan university, in a more sophisticated locale. My students come from very heterogeneous backgrounds in terms of ethnicity, religion and class, but very few of them come from milieus in which values are intact or taken for granted. In other words, whereas the students in the first situation still inhabited a very ordered moral universe, these students exist in a state of near-chaos in terms of meanings, values and identity. They don't know what to believe, how to conduct their lives, or even who they "really" are. I now face a very different kind of responsibility if, on top of the disillusion and relativity in which they already exist, I teach them things that plunge them even further into *anomie*. It seems evident that I face an ethical problem of a different kind, to which I must be attentive if I am not to be grossly irresponsible.

How I respond to this second situation as a responsible teacher (*mutatis mutandis,* the same considerations apply to other activities I may engage in as a sociologist) will depend decisively on my own values.

Assume that I have strong commitments to values, be it on religious or other grounds. This means that I am indeed capable of speaking about values in a capacity *other than* that of sociologist. It seems to us that, in this situation, I have an obligation to make this fact known to my students—not necessarily in the classroom, though it may be appropriate there too. In other words, I must make clear to them that I do not regard the value-free analysis of sociology as the last word about the value dilemmas both they and I face in our ordinary lives. Of course, this does not imply an obligation to "preach" my own values to my students; that is not what the university pays me to do or what they are obliged to listen to. But, in whatever way seems appropriate in my particular setting, I must let the fact shine through that I am a moral individual as well as a sociologist. Another way of saying this is that I must deliberately exercise my "dual citizenship," though I must always make very explicit when I'm speaking *qua* sociologist or in some other capacity—such as the capacity of Christian, politically engaged person, concerned citizen and so on.

It is also possible, of course, that my own moral universe is as disjointed and uncertain as that of my students. In that case, there is no value position that I can let shine through. I can certainly not be required to pretend to have one, just so that my students will be less troubled—that would be not only hypocritical but self-defeating. What I must do then, however, is to make sure that my presentation of sociology does not preclude others from taking value positions that I'm not capable of taking. Minimally, I must reiterate that sociology is not a normative discipline and that people who desire normative guidance will have to look elsewhere I can continue to insist, as we have done in this book, that sociology can be useful to the quest for values in the clarification of options and "if . . . then" scenarios, and of the probable consequence of action.

Our purpose in this book has not been to propose yet another school on sociology—one that, heaven forbid, might call itself the "interpretationist" school or some comparable monstrosity. Rather, we wanted to clarify a common foundation on which different (though clearly not all) existing schools might agree. And while we have strongly reaffirmed the classical ideas of objectivity and value-freeness in the sociological enterprise, we should have dispelled the notion that this implies a stance of detached, cynical observation of a disintegrating society. In line with the classical period in the history of the discipline, we have also reaffirmed the intellectual intention of sociology in gaining a comprehensive view of the modern world, an intention that brings sociology into the immediate neighborhood of other human sciences, notably history, and of philosophy.

Quite apart from possible practical applications of sociology (which, despite our protracted words of caution, we have not repudiated in principle), such a *reprise de conscience* opens up a considerable number of avenues for exploration, some in line with classical concerns and some, as a result of new circumstances, of the nature of innovative departures. Two key phenomena of the modern world are those of individual autonomy and political freedom, both as normative ideals and as partially realized projects. Both still harbor vast problems for sociological analysis. The social context of individual autonomy remains to be explored, a task that brings the sociologist into necessary interaction with both history and psychology. In connection with the latter, there is the fascinating problem of modern identity and its multiple ramifications, and perhaps the development of a new theoretical approach that might be called a *sociological psychology*. There is much room left for the exploration of the social context of political freedom—for instance, the context provided by specific cultural and economic institutions. Sociologists have much work to do yet in interpreting modern values, such as social justice or equality, in their ever-changing meanings in the contemporary world. Of great importance is the sociological critique of all projects of planned social change, be it by way of planning or revolution. There is the vast field of the social and social-psychological dynamics of cultural pluralism, both within and between societies. There are exciting interfaces between sociology and various other sciences (including human biology), and between sociology and various efforts to construct a more adequate philosophical anthropology.

It would be presumptuous to outline here what we would consider to be a hierarchy of priorities in the agenda of sociology. We only mention the above areas of inquiry to indicate that, in our opinion, the task of sociology is by no means completed. Happily, there is a broad middle ground between resting on the achievements of the classics and ignoring them in a concentration on trivia. Put more positively, the intellectual thrust that began with Emile Durkheim, Max Weber and the other giants on whose shoulders we stand has not exhausted itself. Much work remains to be done, in the construction of theory as well as in the accumulation of empirical findings. The method of sociology has not yet become sterile. It still has a promising future.

This book has dealt with method as well as with vocation, thus straddling problems of science and ethics. We have strongly expressed our view of the vocation of sociology as against both technocratic professionalism and ideological pseudoprophecy. Sociology has been and continues to be a vocation with a form of consciousness informed by a specific scientific method, and a vocation carrying its own existential burden. If sociology is to survive in any authentic form, it will be as such a vocation. It stands in an impressive tradition. Though that tradition is not overly long as human history goes, it has proven its validity in an age of exceptional metamorphoses and crisis. If we project that tradition into the future, it is perhaps not presumptuous to suggest that what has emerged since the beginnings of the discipline is something that might well be called a *sociologia perennis* in the continuity and consistency of its intellectual concerns. This book will have fulfilled its purpose if it helps to restore confidence in the viability of such a sociology.

READINGS

In a way, the entire history of sociology is relevant to the argument of this book, so that a massively large body of bibliographical references could plausibly be appended here. This, though, would make little sense, in view of the intended audience as well as of the essayistic character of the book. Instead, what we have done here is to mention a few books that the reader may find useful in following up the discussion in each chapter. In other words, what follows is not a bibliography in the conventional scholarly sense, but a list of books that a reader may take as the starting point of an independent exploration of these issues. We have limited ourselves to books available in English.

For chapter 1

For an earlier statement, by one of us, on the character of the sociological "way of seeing," see Peter L. Berger, *Invitation to Sociology* (Garden City, N.Y., Anchor Books, 1963). On the origins of sociology, particularly in France, see Albert Salomon, *The Tyranny of Progress* (New York, Noonday Press, 1955). For a good overview of current approaches in sociological theory, see Margaret Poloma, *Contemporary Sociological Theory* (New York, Macmillan, 1979).

For chapter 2

Max Weber's methodological writings are still not available *in toto* in English translation, but for a basic understanding of his method of *Verstehen* see Max Weber, *The Methodology of the Social Sciences* (Glencoe, Ill., Free Press, 1949). On Alfred Schutz's approach in general, see his *Collected Papers,* vol. I (The Hague, Nijhoff, 1962). The introduction to that volume, by Maurice Natanson, is still the best available for the reader previously unacquainted with Schutz. Of particular importance for the issues discussed in this chapter is Schutz's *Reflections on the Problem of Relevance* (New Haven, Yale University Press, 1970). The following are useful on the general relation between sociology and phenomenology: Maurice Natanson (ed.), *Phenomenology and the Social Sciences,* 2 vols. (Evanston, Ill., Northwestern University Press, 1973); George Psathas (ed.), *Phenomenological Sociology* (New York, Wiley, 1973); Thomas Luckmann (ed.), *Phenomenology and Sociology* (Harmondsworth, Middlesex, Penguin Books, 1978). A very useful book, written from a more positivistic viewpoint but strongly influenced by phenomenology, continues to be Felix Kaufmann, *Methodology of the Social Sciences* (New York, Oxford University Press, 1944).

For chapter 3

At the core of the discussion of this chapter, of course, is the so-called sociology of knowledge. For the development of this subdiscipline, see the following: Werner Stark, *The Sociology of Knowledge* (Glencoe, Ill., Free Press, 1958); James Curtis and John Petras (eds.), *The Sociology of Knowledge* (New York, Praeger, 1970); Gunter Remmling (ed.), *Towards the Sociology of Knowledge* (London, Routledge & Kegan Paul, 1973). Max Scheler's basic work in this area is, to our knowledge, still untranslated, but see John Staude, *Max Scheler* (New York, Free Press, 1967). On Karl Mannheim, see his *Ideology and Utopia* (London, Routledge & Kegan Paul, 1936) and *Essays on the Sociology of Knowledge* (New York, Oxford University Press, 1952). For an attempt to apply Schutzian ideas to the sociology of knowledge, see Peter L. Berger and Thomas Luckmann, *The Social Construction of Reality* (Garden City, N.Y., Doubleday, 1966).

For chapter 4

On the general problem of how to reconcile a philosophical anthropology with social-scientific notions of "boundedness," see Maurice Natanson, *The Journeying Self* (Reading, Mass., Addison-Wesley, 1970). The *loci classici* for, respectively, external and internal "boundedness," are Emile Durkheim, *The Rules of Sociological Method* (Glencoe, Ill., Free Press, 1938), and George Herbert Mead, *Mind, Self and Society* (Chicago, University of Chicago Press, 1934). For commentaries on these two authors, see Steven Lukes, *Emile Durkheim* (London, Allen Lane, 1973); Robert Nisbet, *The Sociology of Emile Durkheim* (New York, Oxford University Press, 1974); Maurice Natanson, *The Social Dynamics of George Herbert Mead* (Washington, Public Affairs Press, 1956). On the tyrannical potential of Enlightenment rationality, see J. L. Talmon, *The Origins of Totalitarian Democracy* (New York, Praeger, 1968). On Max Weber's view of the relation of rationality, science and history, see a very instructive recent work: Guenther Roth and Wolfgang Schluchter, *Max Weber's Vision of History* (Berkeley, University of California Press, 1979).

For chapter 5

On the carryover of technological thought patterns to other areas of life, see Peter L. Berger, Brigitte Berger and Hansfried Kellner, *The Homeless Mind: Modernization and Consciousness* (New York, Random House, 1973). That book contains our fullest statement to date of the relation between modernization and consciousness. On the recent discussion over the new "knowledge class," see B. Bruce-Briggs (ed.), *The New Class?* (New Brunswick, N.J., Transaction Books, 1979), and Alvin Gouldner, *The Future of Intellectuals and the Rise of the New Class* (New York, Seabury, 1979). On sociology as an effort at "theodicy," see Ernest Becker, *The Structure of Evil* (New York, Braziller, 1968). The literature on the relation between Marxism and social science is, of course, astronomical in expanse. A recent work presumably marks a certain culmination in the critical evaluation of Marxism: Leszek Kolakowski, *Main Currents of Marxism,* 3 vols. (Oxford, Clarendon Press, 1978).

For chapter 6

On the general question of the "crisis of modernity," we would refer again to our previously cited *The Homeless Mind*. In classical sociology, Vilfredo Pareto comes closest to having developed a theory of decadence, in his *The Mind and Society,* 2 vols. (New York, Dover, 1963). For a useful selection from this monumental opus, see S. E. Finer (ed.), *Vilfredo Pareto: Sociological Writings* (New York, Praeger, 1966). The first of Arnold Gehlen's works to appear in English translation is his *Man in the Age of Technology* (New York, Columbia University Press, 1980). For an interesting discussion of modern consciousness, strongly influenced by Gehlen, see Anton Zijderveld, *On Clichés: The Supersedure of Meaning by Function in Modernity* (London, Routledge & Kegan Paul, 1979).

INDEX